Advance Praise for *MORE! The Microdose Diet*

"*The Microdose Diet* is a precise yet artful exploration of how to transform your life and your leadership through microdosing. Peggy has spent years cultivating her protocol, which blends psychedelic science with best practices in mindfulness to deliver lifelong change. As an investor in the mental health and longevity space, I can say for certain that this book is a superb introduction to holistic microdosing, and is a critical addition to a growing body of work on the transformational effects of psychedelic science."

— Garri Zmudze, General Partner, LongeVC

"Peggy's simple, straightforward approach to this medicine is a refreshing and uniquely approachable combination of professionalism, compassion and leadership. It's rare to find someone with Peggy's corporate pedigree who is able to seamlessly bridge access to a whole new way of healing and showing up in this world without pushing unnecessary dogma or unrealistic protocols. The Microdose Diet will help so many people!"

— Tracey Tee, Founder & Steward, Moms on Mushrooms

"*The Microdose Diet* pioneers a revolutionary approach to wellness, self-discovery and personal transformation! Combining the meticulous art of microdosing psilocybin, with an array of synergistic alternative therapy tools, Peggy delivers a comprehensive protocol that is poised to enlighten

and empower individuals on their microdosing journey to self-improvement."

— Donald Gauvreau, MSc.,
Founder & CEO, Conscious Mind Clinic

"*The Microdose Diet* is a must read for any leader interested in microdosing. Peggy's protocol, nurtured over years, seamlessly merges psychedelic science with mindfulness, ensuring enduring change. As an entrepreneur and owner of microdosing brand Bien, I can attest that this book is a stellar introduction to holistic microdosing. It is a pivotal addition to the growing body of work on the transformative impact of psychedelic science."

— Suzanne KHAN, CEO, Bien.health

"Are you seeking a comprehensive guide to microdosing psilocybin? Peggy's *The Microdose Diet* is an insightful resource that delves deep into the holistic microdosing protocol. Ideal for both beginners and experienced individuals interested in microdosing psilocybin, *The Microdose Diet* offers a mindful approach, emphasizing the importance of mindset, setting, and intention in microdosing practices, ensuring that readers are well-equipped to use psilocybin most beneficially.

Beyond the thorough coverage of preparation and integration processes in microdosing, Peggy meticulously covers critical aspects such as dosage, scheduling, and setting intentions, providing readers with a detailed framework for their microdosing journey. Furthermore, Peggy introduces readers to a range of supportive tools such as journaling, tapping, and guided visualization, tools designed to enhance the microdosing experience.

The Microdose Diet is an excellent guide that balances scientific insight with practical advice. It's a must-read for anyone interested in exploring the transformative potential of microdosing in a controlled manner."

— Josh Kerbel and Jon Kamin,
Co-founders, Frshminds.com

"*The Microdose Diet* protocol is a must for professionals looking to gain performance, focus, creativity and mood edge in an increasingly competitive environment where balanced decisions from a position of strength will further distinguish one from the crowd. This is the best asymmetric trade now—all upside and no downside."

— Maxim Sytchev, Managing Director,
National Bank Financial

More! The Microdose Diet

The Microdose Diet

THE 90-DAY PLAN FOR MORE SUCCESS, PASSION, AND HAPPINESS

PEGGY VAN DE PLASSCHE

A SAVIO REPUBLIC BOOK
An Imprint of Post Hill Press
ISBN: 979-8-88845-358-2
ISBN (eBook): 979-8-88845-359-9

MORE! The Microdose Diet:
The 90-Day Plan for More Success, Passion, and Happiness

Cover Photo by Jeremie Dupont

posthillpress.com
New York • Nashville
Published in the United States of America

1 2 3 4 5 6 7 8 9 10

Contents

MORE! – Where It All Begins

If I had to select one word to describe the central theme of my life, it would be ***more.***

A yearning for ***more*** began at an early age. I was born in the '70s and grew up in a small industrial town in France, where girls, especially the ones from low socioeconomic backgrounds, were taught to be invisible. My parents were uneducated and my mother struggled to raise my older brother and I by herself while facing financial and mental health challenges. The latter was amplified after my brother's untimely passing in an accident. You might assume that with a difficult upbringing, I would have been content to fade into the backdrop. But for whatever reason, I was born with plenty of drive and ambition and always knew that I wanted ***more*** out of life than what the cards I had been dealt supposedly predisposed me to have. I was a six-foot tall woman that my parents, society, and church had tried hard to fold into a three-foot long box. I ached to get out and see what sort of world I could shape for myself.

I went to a top-tier business school in France that I financed via death, debt, and odd jobs. The insurance settlement I received from my brother's accident allowed me to finance my first two years of schooling, while the following three years were funded by student debt and odd jobs. These included rollerblading in short-shorts with a giant cigarette attached to my back, registering guests for bar openings, and everything in between. Thanks to Oliver Stone and his movie *Wall Street*, **my goal had always been to work in finance in North America, which I considered to be the ultimate success symbol.** As with most things in my life, I was told that it was not going to happen for me.

After considerable time and effort, I finally landed an accounting job in Montreal, Canada. I was in! For the next decade, I focused on climbing the corporate ladder—even when it meant ending a relationship with my French fiancé who couldn't relate to or keep up with my constant work and travel. By the time I met my second fiancé (a fellow finance buff and match made in heaven), I had been fully sucked into the classic trope of North American corporate life: high stress, high expectations, high salary. I was working eighty hours per week like the cold-blooded machine I had seen in the movies growing up, and I was delighted about it. **I was a well-paid corporate woman, worlds away from the small town I had grown up in.**

There were single years that felt like twenty and I fired more people than I can count. In the process, I also invested hundreds of millions in real estate and tech companies and earned my stripes as a bona fide finance expert. I spoke in front of huge audiences all over the world, advised boards of top financial institutions, but still, **I had not been able to find my *more*, this zest**

for life, nor the recipe for success that I so desperately craved. Like many people, I was living in a state of constant anxiety and was addicted to work, emails, texts, and alcohol (and sugar!) that numbed the pain while filling the emptiness. I may have had a natural tendency for these behaviors, but the environment I was in dramatically amplified the symptoms.

Health conscious and hesitant to start taking anti-anxiety or anti-depression prescription drugs to lift the constant dark cloud over my head, I tried mainstream (and even slightly "woo woo") strategies to reclaim the life I knew I could have, reach my potential, and finally claim this elusive ***more***. Psychotherapy, coaching, tapping, meditation, visualization, energy healing, acupuncture, Mexican sweat lodge, craniosacral, homeopathy, positive affirmation.... I experimented with them all. Still, nothing had quite been able to penetrate the walls of protection, negativity, and self-hatred I had built up throughout the course of my life. **I could not seem to get out of my own way.**

As I was on the verge of reaching out for a medical prescription, I came across multiple articles on microdosing psilocybin through trusted publications such as *The Economist, The WSJ, Financial Times* (and also *Harper's Bazaar*!). It piqued my interest and I did what I do best—I went to work!

After extensive research, the recent scientific studies and changes in legislation led me to experiment with microdosing psilocybin. The fact that conservative organizations such as the US and Canadian Department of Veterans Affairs had launched clinical trials to study the benefits of psychedelics as mental health treatment for veterans convinced me that there was something there. And the billions in capital that have been allocated to the psychedelics industry by savvy investors and business experts confirmed my analysis.

I have always been skeptical toward prescribed drugs related to mental health. I could see how they could help someone get out of a dire state of mind by putting a band-aid on symptoms. But I personally had no interest whatsoever in being dependent on a drug—prescribed or not—for the rest of my life. **What I wanted was to treat the cause of the problem, not its symptoms.** Psychedelics do just that. They don't treat the symptoms; instead, they rewire the brain. By creating new pathways in the brain, psilocybin addresses the root cause. That is what I was after.

To be clear, microdosing psilocybin was not a decision I approached lightly. I had never taken recreational nor prescribed drugs before, but I liked that psilocybin is plant-based and free from chemical manipulations. I pored over online testimonials and studied research to understand the appropriate regimen.

There was a sliver of nervousness the first time I microdosed; **the moment I knew I was ready was when the hopefulness I felt overshadowed the nerves.** I had done extensive due diligence and believed that psilocybin might just be the thing to help create the sense of "more" I had been after all my life.

The benefits of this decision have surpassed my wildest dreams. For the first time in my life, the undercurrent of tension that seemed to permeate my very existence has been erased. The adjectives that I now claim as my own—relaxed, creative, focused, joyful, positive—would have been incomprehensible to past Peggy. It truly feels like every facet of my life has been upleveled. I'm sleeping better with no more of the catastrophic nightmares that plagued me for decades, my relationships are stronger as I'm more present in my daily life, I'm more willing to try new things, career interactions and networking events fill me with excitement rather than dread… I could keep going. **In a nutshell, I am now feeling alive, excited about things to come, capable**

of peacefully addressing anything, and confident that *even more* is on the way!

Microdosing psilocybin has truly been a blessing. However, **what really brought me to the next level was the strategic combination of alternative medicines:** journaling, tapping, visualization, meditation, and psychedelics. None of these tools alone were able to permeate my shell, but together the results have been nothing short of extraordinary. From the publication of the book you have in your hands, to the launch of The Microdose Diet platform, my career, finances, and life have totally transformed.

Seeing the effect it had on me, many have started The Microdose Diet as well. Others have seen the same value in The Microdose Diet protocol, where things that had been blocked, seemingly forever, finally started manifesting. It brings me a great deal of happiness to see them start to unlock their lives, and I credit this process with making it possible for the small but growing community of people who have taken back control of their lives. You are now one of these people. **I am wishing you tremendous success in getting *more* out of your life; a new chapter begins!**

Learn more about me and The Microdose Diet by scanning the QR code below.

Introduction

This is not a book about psychedelics.

This is a book about success and how to get *more* of it. This book is the step 0 for anything you are aiming for—a promotion, a new job or business, more revenues, additional skills, and so on—anything professional, but also personal.

The definition of success varies widely from person to person, location to location, and era to era. Success is anchored in Maslow's hierarchy of needs, from physiological needs to self-actualization. However, in Western societies, money and career achievements have replaced other avenues of becoming successful.

However, no man is an island; nothing is an island. **Your professional success is using the same foundation as your personal success.** If you don't feel worthy, if you have social anxiety, or if your nervous system is fried, this will negatively impact both your professional and personal affairs.

Being a professional myself, I made the decision to use career success as an entry point for The Microdose Diet. The topic could have been personal finance, relationships, or weight.

These topics will be addressed in subsequent books. The method and process will stay the same for all the areas of your life you want to experience more success in. I will change the exercises, but the underlying philosophy is a constant; it has been built on two decades of intense research. Today, with this book, you will get ancillary benefits in all the areas of your life from the work you will be doing now on career success.

You will find information on psychedelics, not because this is a book on psychedelics, but because **microdosing psilocybin is an important tool in your toolkit and this warrants more explanation** than the traditional mindset work of affirmations or meditation. After reading this book, you will know enough to be dangerous when it comes to the topic of psychedelics, but it is absolutely not my intention to make you an "expert" on psychedelics. Many books have been written on that topic, albeit very dry books, and they will give you all the information you need, should you decide to go in that direction. What I intend to do with this book is to give you the tools and protocols you need to kick off your microcode diet and start seeing the benefits in your life today.

But let's begin first with some free association with the term "magic mushrooms." What comes to mind?

Maybe a 1970s-era rockstar tripping for fun and creative inspiration after a show?

Perhaps a group of long-haired, free-spirited guys zoned out on a beach somewhere?

Or someone locked away for committing a federal offense?

I'm here to flip those stereotypes on their head. Based on the stigmas that exist, I might be the last person you would expect to use magic mushrooms. A former banker and venture capitalist, I have allocated hundreds of millions to tech and real estate investments, led innovation for a large financial institution, and launched several companies. As you might imagine, I'm very type-A and have always been focused on doing "the right thing." Health is of paramount importance to me. I'm an avid tennis player and yoga practitioner and I am very cautious about putting as few chemicals as possible into my body. But **microdosing magic mushrooms—also known as psilocybin—has become a critical part of my healing and wellness journey.**

Like many in today's society, I had been climbing the corporate ladder for decades and had become entrenched in a never-ending cycle of anxiety and depression. I was addicted to my email and obsessed with getting ahead in the hustle culture. To protect myself from falling apart (or having a complete meltdown), I had built up walls around my authentic desires and real emotions until not even I could recognize them. I was also self-medicating with alcohol and sugar in an attempt to take the edge off the intense anxiety, anger, and self-hatred that simmered right under the surface. **I had become completely numb, just passively going through the motions of my life.**

For years, I desperately tried every method under the sun to get me to *feel something*: preferably a positive emotion like joy, excitement, or hope. Therapy, meditation, tapping, coaching, energy healing, you name it… I spent countless hours and massive amounts of money trying to dig myself out of the grave in which I had been buried alive. It felt like there was this constant tug of war between what I had and what I truly wanted out of life. Compounding that unease was a deep sense of guilt. Here I was with what many would consider a dream life. What right did I have to be so unfulfilled?

When I finally reached my breaking point and was about ready to turn to pharmaceutical help (what I considered my

very last resort), I came across microdosing. Skeptical at first due to the legal gray area and social stigma, I dove deep into education in an attempt to learn as much as possible. What I eventually understood was compelling. Psychedelics like psilocybin have been used for thousands of years. They do not lead to physical dependence and can be produced naturally. Mushrooms should realistically not even be in the same category as substances like LSD or MDMA, which are synthetic and can vary widely in their quality and effect. What's more, there is a world of difference between the "trips" that are most commonly associated with psychedelics and what happens during microdosing. In most cases, drinking a cup of coffee will produce a more noticeable physical reaction than taking a microdose of psilocybin.

When it comes to the business opportunities linked with psychedelics, many are starting to wake up and take notice. The **market value for psychedelics is projected to grow from $2 billion in 2020 to $10.75 billion by 2027**; accordingly, savvy investors and businesspeople have been busy developing new companies and investment funds to capture the profits. Similar to how marijuana was initially shunned due to a lack of education and understanding from the public, psilocybin has suffered from a reputation that is beginning to be turned upside down.

Thanks to the twenty years I spent as a seeker, I had extensive experience with modalities such as tapping, meditation, Neuro Linguistic Programming, hypnosis and so on. Uniting all my knowledge together, **I combined microdosing psychedelics with alternative therapies in order to strategically rewire my brain, heal my emotional wounds, calm my nervous system, and reach my goals.** This protocol is called The Microdose Diet. It has changed my life, starting with my career and finances where my main focus was for so long. My life at large has also benefited from this process.

I am now at peace and feel that I have regained my rightful place in the driver's seat of my own life. No longer am I asleep at the wheel or mindlessly watching the landscape go by through the open window. Knowing that my experience could help others and serve to destigmatize the use of psychedelics, I decided to formalize and share this protocol. This book is the result of hundreds of hours of research, experiments, and analysis. I know it will change your world for the better. And this is just the beginning.

The Microdose Diet is for you if you're eager to unlock your full potential and discover a sense of joy and fulfillment that you may not have believed possible. It isn't necessarily about prompting big external changes (unless you choose to do so), but rather about feeling, thinking, and acting more like the best, truest, and most authentic version of yourself. After the ninety days, you will be blown away by what your life feels and looks like when taken off autopilot. **From increased performance and enhanced well-being to better relationships and elevated awareness, there are no limitations to what you can achieve through this process.**

After people find out I microdose mushrooms, their eyes widen and they almost always start firing off a list of questions:

How much do you take?
Do you use it every day?
Are there side effects?
How long does it take to notice a difference?
How do I make sure that the rewiring of my brain is positive?

How can I control what I want to rewire my brain with?

***The Microdose Diet* is intended to answer these questions by providing a clear framework for you to begin your own strategic transformation journey, including microdosing as one of the tools in the toolkit.** I call this ninety-day program a "diet" for a specific reason. Think of other diets you know: Atkins, paleo, keto, vegan, and so on. None of these would work identically for every single individual out there; we all have unique biological factors, environments, lifestyles, and preferences. However, there are fundamentals that *do* work for everyone: eat whole foods rather than those that are processed, get enough vitamins and nutrients, and consume the calories that your body needs to thrive.

Similarly, **the program I describe in this book is intended to give you the education and methodology to confidently go off on your own.** The results you will experience might differ slightly from your friends, relatives, and coworkers, but you will **achieve great outcomes**

By combining two of the most powerful alternative medicines—microdosing psilocybin and tapping—in an easy, fast and simple ninety-day protocol, The Microdose Diet **creates life-changing results.** Strategically harnessing the ability of psilocybin to rewire the brain and tapping to inform the brain what to rewire it with, The Microdose Diet is more than just another mindset book: it is a **clear, scientifically-backed recipe for success.** You will learn all about tapping and microdosing in section 1 "Your Psychedelic Education". Feel free to jump there now if you want a sneak peek ahead of time!

While following The Microdose Diet and throughout your life, I encourage you to question everything you read,

think, hear, and say. What if the things you have been told to believe are not true? What if you didn't have to believe what your mind is telling you? Become the best investigator of the most fascinating topic: yourself!

Follow me on YouTube to get more insights on how to find more professional and personal success with The Microdose Diet.

Section 1

Your Psychedelic Education

Chapter 1

Why You Should Care about The Microdose Diet

Think back to what it was like to be a young child, before you learned to be jaded and protect yourself from feeling pain. What was it like to experience the world that way? How big were your dreams? How great was your joy? **The Microdose Diet is the key to regaining the zest for life that many of us have lost over time.** With your mojo back, you will reach the heights of success you are aiming for, while having a pleasant experience doing so. What more could one ask for?

1) THE MICRODOSE DIET WORKS

My newfound (or re-found) ability to experience life with curiosity, gusto, and optimism has upleveled not just the big

moments (like giving important presentations or having difficult conversations), but also my day-to-day life.

As a simple example, I used to order the same meal each time I went out to eat with only very slight variations based on the restaurant. I thought nothing of it until after I started microdosing and suddenly appreciated the variety that existed right in front of me. For the first time in a long time, I didn't default to the choice I had programmed myself to make. In a way, it's like those game shows where the host asks contestants to decide between a set of doors in an effort to win the best prize. For years, I only saw one door, and the prize wasn't that great. With microdosing, the first door still existed, but so did many others. And I was actually *excited* about what was waiting behind them.

The Microdose Diet is not a treatment; **it's a protocol to unlearn negative patterns and reprogram the way your brain process information**. It doesn't erase anything you already have, but rather *adds* more opportunities for neural connection. We gain the ability to stop and think about how the "best version of ourselves" would behave in a given circumstance and then move forward and act accordingly. This return to your authentic, bold, limitless self is really the goal of microdosing psilocybin.

"Things that had been stuck for a long time have started to manifest." J.G.

2) THE MICRODOSE DIET WILL CHANGE YOUR LIFE (IF YOU FOLLOW THE PROGRAM!)

If you were to meet a genie who would grant you your desired life now, what would it be? I am pretty sure that, between us of course, **your dream life would look wildly different**. Maybe you would have a different spouse or no spouse at all, maybe a different career in another country; it would most likely be fun, prosperous, bold, and you'd be The (Wo)Man.

I used to fantasize about waking up amnesic, not knowing that I was fearful, playing small, and that I'd have the opportunity to reinvent myself as I dreamt I could be: daring, fun-loving, confident, joyful, successful, lucky, wealthy, and so on. It was not so much my conditions that I was disappointed by, but myself. **Living my life half-way, stuck in conditioning, limiting beliefs, fears, and pains of the past.** My story was my prized gold cage. On one hand, it was keeping me stuck, but on the other hand, I was attached to it. I was in love with success and achievements, as well as with my pain and grief. I was trapped. Physically, mentally, and emotionally.

In just a few months, and with limited time and effort, I was able to achieve things I had dreamt of, but had never been able to do: writing a book, finding a great literary agent, being professionally published, starting a new business, but also releasing past neuroses, tremendous levels of anxiety, stress, depression, and hopelessness. **I am now more relaxed than I have ever been while at the same time being more productive.**

If this resonates with you, and I am 100 percent convinced that it does, then **you need to learn about** microdosing psilocybin, and more importantly, the combination of microdosing with tapping, journaling, visualization, and guided meditation, which is **The Microdose Diet.**

3) THE MICRODOSE DIET IS THE ONLY HOLISTIC APPROACH OUT THERE

The triumvirate of mind-body-emotions is the cornerstone of The Microdose Diet, making The Microdose Diet the precursor to any type of personal or professional development.

Without this building block, the results you will see, regardless of the amount of time, energy, and money you allocate to these programs, will be, at best, underwhelming.

I have been a seeker all my life and have spent a tremendous amount of effort to better myself. However, when I look back at all that labor, I wish I had started at the beginning—**working concurrently on my unconscious and conscious mind, my body and nervous system, and my emotions**. The results would have been exponentially better in a fraction of the time.

This is what you are doing with The Microdose Diet.

a. The Unconscious and Conscious Mind

In the 1910s, Sigmund Freud, the founding father of psychoanalysis, brought forth his "Theory of the Mind," arguing that **the mind was to be divided into the conscious and the unconscious.**[1] The unconscious, which refers to the mental processes of which individuals are unaware, is believed to take the lion's share of our minds, while the conscious mind refers to what an individual is aware of—their daily, waking thoughts and emotions. Importantly, the unconscious includes that which is actively repressed from conscious thought (versus all that is not unconscious).

Most of us are well aware of the importance of the unconscious mind. However, we also spend most of our time working on our "mindset," the conscious part of our mind. Irrational, isn't it? Best case scenario, **we have been wasting our time focusing on improving our conscious thoughts that will be overridden by our unconscious at the first opportunity.** Worst case scenario, **we have been reinforcing our unconscious beliefs; indeed, every time we have been writing, speaking, or thinking positive affirmations**, such as "I am happy and successful," or "I am the CEO of JPMC [replace with the company of your choice]," your subconscious mind has been reinforcing the thought that "No, dumbass, you are not happy, nor are you the CEO of JPMC, Jamie Dimon is, and you are just a VP, Innovation at CIBC," for example.

In order to be working on mindset successfully, our unconscious beliefs need to be taken care of first and foremost. Let's say that you are coming from a blue-collar family and you have been fed the very common belief that "People like us can't be successful," "Better to have a solid family than money," "Rich people are thieves," and so on, your likelihood to displace Jamie Dimon is pretty slim, as it represents everything you have unconsciously internalized as "bad."

In The Microdose Diet, you will work on these unconscious beliefs first to make space in your hard drive. **Only then can we address the conscious aspect of your mind by implanting supportive beliefs that are congruent with your goals.**

> **"The mind is like an iceberg, it floats with one seventh of its bulk above water."**
> **–Sigmund Freud**

b. The Mind-Body Connection

Our physical health impacts our mental and conscious states, including our emotions and behaviors; reciprocally, our mental health impacts our physical well-being. This interconnectedness of our minds and bodies is referred as the "mind-body connection." It is enabled through various communication networks between our brain and the neurological, endocrine, and immune systems of our body.[2]

A very important piece of this mind-body connection is our nervous system.

Calming the nervous system is one of the three key components of The Microdose Diet (in addition to reprogramming the unconscious mind with deliberate beliefs and healing emotional wounds). **When you are in fight-flight-freeze mode, your auto-pilot kicks in, making it impossible for you to take the best actions for yourself.**

By recalibrating your nervous system to a calmer state, you now have the opportunity to **fully collaborate with your mind** (unconscious and conscious), **versus going to pre-programmed, limiting patterns of thoughts and actions** (or rather reactions).

c. Healing Emotional Wounds

We all have numerous emotional wounds, old and new, deep and shallow. **These unhealed emotional wounds lurk in the background, ready to make us unconscious, defaulting to our auto-pilot, our fight-flight-freeze answer.**

Whether **these wounds** are massive—abandonment, rejection, humiliation, betrayal, or neglect from our caregivers—or not, **they impact our lives and careers in more ways than we can imagine.**

The failure to perform well at a school play or on the debate team might leave us with social anxiety, less than optimal public speaking abilities, and create setbacks in our careers.

An unstable home can trigger hyper-vigilant behaviors, making it difficult to trust people, and preventing us from bonding with coworkers and friends.

As Gabor Maté mentions in his excellent book, *The Myth of Normal,* **trauma is not what happens to you. Trauma is what happens inside you as a result of what happens to you.**[3] Which means that the wound can be healed (and should be healed).

If you want to live a full life, in the driver seat versus on the passenger seat, healing your emotional wounds is a prerequisite, as well as calming your body and reprogramming your limiting beliefs. If only one or two aspects of this triumvirate are addressed, changes will not be long-term and your well-being—mental and physical—are not guaranteed (or rather, it is guaranteed that you won't have the well-being you deserve). Like a stool with two legs, you might be able to keep it stable for a while with a lot of effort and willpower, but eventually it will collapse, and you with it.

> **"Every time you are tempted to react in the same old way, ask yourself if you want to be a prisoner of the past or a pioneer of the future."**
> **–Deepak Chopra**

4) THE MICRODOSE DIET COMBINES THE BEST TECHNOLOGIES

The same way development programs focus on one aspect of changes (body or mind or emotions), they only use one tool to do so. Whether these tools are meditation, hypnosis, or affirmations, they are very unidimensional and single-minded.

It is well understood that if you want to be a great tennis player, you will benefit from a combination of weight training, yoga, stretching, sleeping, mindful eating, in addition to practicing the actual game of tennis.

However, when it comes to personal and professional development, often only one tool is used—and it's most often geared toward the conscious mind. Then we wonder why the results are underwhelming!

It took me fifteen years to develop The Microdose Diet, using myself (and my relatives) as the guinea pigs. It took me fifteen years to understand that **to create repeatable, scalable, long-lasting changes, I needed to use multiple technologies on my mind (conscious and unconscious), body, and emotions.**

One plus one equals three, and in the context of The Microdose Diet, equals infinity. **There is no limit to the changes you can generate.** I experienced more results in a few months of using The Microdose Diet than with years of development programs.

Again, we are well-aware of the **exponential results coming from multi-pronged approaches in many disciplines**, such as sports, however, we have been stuck on a one-track approach when it comes to the most important aspect of our lives: personal development.

a. Microdosing Psilocybin

Microdosing psilocybin on its own is extremely helpful to **calm your nervous system and lower your ego barriers.**

By calming your nervous system, you can create some space in your body, mind, and spirit. Most of us (all of us) run around in our daily lives with an overtaxed nervous system—meaning in fight, flight, or freeze. And then we wonder why we don't seem to be able to reach higher levels of success and happiness in our lives. But **when we don't have any room to take in any additional**

tasks, discussions, or pressures on top of what we already have in our day-to-day lives, it is impossible to expand.

Think about it—if you want bigger opportunities in your life, such as growing your business, getting a promotion or a raise, or growing your audience on social media, you will face multiple obstacles: difficult discussions with your boss or employees, rejections from investors or clients, criticism from trolls and haters. Hence you will need to up your game. And if your nervous system is overloaded (which is the case for most of us from the get-go) it will not deal well with the added tensions coming from the difficult discussions and challenges that will inevitably come up. So you end up being stuck and depressed because you want more from your life, but can't seem to get it. Even if this "more from life" might mean enjoying life as it is now, with no desire for more growth. Bottom line, you need to make space for better, bigger things, and for that to happen, **you need to be able to handle more. Hence the need for a calmer nervous system.**

By lowering your ego defenses, **microdosing psilocybin will also enable you to more easily access your unconscious**. First, to understand what might be the programs running in the background consuming your CPU (energy) and leading you in the wrong direction (hello, conditioning, limiting beliefs, and emotional wounds). Second, to rewrite these programs with empowering messages congruent with your desired goals and outcomes.

I will explain microdosing in more detail in chapter four of this section.

b. Tapping, Journaling, Visualization, and Guided Meditation

Tapping, havening, journaling, visualization, and guided meditation are the tools we use to upgrade your operating system and rewrite your software. **The combination of all these technologies is what makes The Microdose Diet unique: it addresses the body, mind, and emotions via a multipronged approach.** Mindset work alone is never enough; your body and nervous system will override it at the first opportunity. The body and nervous system are not enough either, as they don't give any instruction to your subconscious regarding the direction it should go. Same with emotions—healing past wounds is a requirement, but in parallel, the mind needs to be given new instructions and the body needs to be calmed.

I will explain tapping, journaling, visualization, and guided meditation in more detail in chapter five.

• • • • •

If you properly follow The Microdose Diet, **you will witness tremendous results in your life.** This program can be applied to anything you want: career, money, health, weight, or relationships.

This is why you should care about microdosing and The Microdose Diet! I have zero doubt that if you picked up this book, you are like me, and you want MORE! out of your life. **Go beyond the perceived blocks and limitations of your current life.** If you follow The Microdose Diet, a new world will open up before you.

However, for this to happen, you will have to do the work. Just microdosing is not enough. I know we all want the magic, easy pill and this program is as close to it as it comes—**only fifteen minutes a day to discover a new you and new life is, in the grand scheme of things, the smallest investment you will ever make for yourself for such results.** Think about it, you spend more time taking your shower, going to the bathroom or making coffee every day. So there is no reason for you not to allocate this time to yourself. And if you don't seem capable, then BOOM!, it means that deep down your fear of change and lack of self-love is bigger than you think, two things we address in The Microdose Diet. So an even bigger reason for you to buckle up!

A day on The Microdose Diet.

Key Takeaways - Chapter 1

- The Microdose Diet is a program to **unlearn negative patterns and reprogram the way your brain process information.**
- "Things that had been **stuck for a long time** have **started to manifest.**" J.G.
- **Your dream life looks wildly different** than your current circumstances.
- From being stuck in **conditioning, limiting beliefs, fears and pains of the past to being in the flow, relaxed, and open.**
- The triumvirate of **mind-body-emotions** is the cornerstone of The Microdose Diet, working concurrently **on your unconscious and conscious mind, your body and nervous system, and your emotions.**
- You have been **wasting** your **time focusing on improving your conscious thoughts** that will be **overridden by your unconscious** at the first opportunity.
- To **successfully change** your mindset, your **unconscious beliefs** need to be taken care of **first and foremost.**
- Your **physical health impacts your mental and conscious states**, including your emotions and behaviors, and reciprocally, your **mental health impacts** your **physical well-being.**
- When **you are in fight-flight-freeze mode**, your auto-pilot kicks in, making it **impossible** for you **to take the best actions for yourself.**
- By recalibrating your **nervous system to a calmer state**, you now have the opportunity to **fully collaborate with**

your mind, versus going to **pre-programmed limiting patterns of thoughts and (re)actions.**

- **Unhealed emotional wounds** lurk in the background, ready to make you **unconscious**, defaulting to your **auto-pilot**, your **fight-flight-freeze answer.**
- Unhealed emotional wounds **negatively impact your lives and careers** in more ways than you can imagine.
- If you want to **live a full life, healing your emotional wounds** is a **pre-requisite**; as are **calming your body** and **reprogramming your limiting beliefs.**
- The Microdose Diet **combines the best technologies** to harness the exponential results coming from **a multi-pronged approach.**
- **Microdosing psilocybin** is extremely helpful to **calm your nervous system and lower your ego barriers**, helping you **access your unconscious mind.**
- Tapping, havening, journaling, visualization, and guided meditation are the tools you will use to upgrade your operating system and rewrite your software. **The combination** of all these technologies is what makes **The Microdose Diet unique: it addresses the body, mind, and emotions via a multipronged approach.**
- In fifteen minutes a day, you will witness **tremendous results** and go **beyond the perceived blocks and limitations** of your current life.

Chapter 2
What Are Psychedelics?

The word "psychedelics" can be quite intimidating. Most people's minds jump immediately to intense experiences—things like ayahuasca retreats or raves where everyone is on MDMA—that they've read about or seen on TV. The reality is much more nuanced than that.

When I describe psychedelics to curious friends or clients, I start with the fact that they can either be **plant-based or chemically-produced**. Psilocybin, along with cannabis (yes, weed can be considered a psychedelic!) and ayahuasca are the best-known categories of plant-based psychedelics. This was critically important to me when I began my own microdosing journey. I knew I wanted something natural to avoid quality variation and flooding my body with chemicals. I don't even take painkillers when I have a headache, so I *certainly* wasn't about to start experimenting with something like Ketamine or MDMA which are produced in a lab. I ultimately decided to **use psilocybin not only because it's plant-based, but also because it's widely accessible and very well-priced.**

Psychedelics give us the ability to take advantage of a concept called neuroplasticity, which became popularized after Dr. Eric Kandel won the Nobel Prize in 2000 for his work on the topic. Neuroplasticity refers to the fact that our brains are not static organs; in fact, they are ever-changing in response to stimuli. Put very simply, this means that **it really is possible to rewire our brains.** Think about it like this: imagine you're walking through the forest following a little trail. This is your brain using its existing neural connections. Now envision a team of lumberjacks who come in and clear paths so you can easily access new parts of the forest—areas you never would have been able to reach before without tremendous effort. That is essentially what psychedelics are doing in the brain. Functional MRI scans have shown that **psilocybin and its family members actually change the brain's connectivity patterns.**

But let's start with the basics!

1) DEFINITION

Psychedelics, also called serotonergic hallucinogens, are powerful **psychoactive substances**, meaning they **affect how the brain works and cause changes in mood, awareness, thoughts, feelings, or behavior.**[4]

Alcohol, caffeine, nicotine, marijuana, and certain pain medicines are also psychoactive substances.[5] Yes, your morning cup of coffee is a psychoactive substance that alters perception and mood and affects numerous cognitive processes!

As per the National Library of Medicine definition, **psychedelics are generally considered physiologically safe and do not lead to dependence or addiction.**[6]

2) HISTORY

Psychedelics have a long history of use by Indigenous peoples of the Americas, specifically Turtle Island, including the Mazatec, Huichol, Shipibo, and other nations as well as the pre-Columbian Maya, Olmec, Zapotec, and Aztec societies.

Due to the extensive historical use of psychedelics in religious contexts, Dr. Jerome H. Jaffe, a Clinical Professor of Psychiatry at the University of Maryland School of Medicine, defines psychedelics as "a type of drug **capable of reliably bringing about states of altered perception, thought, and feeling that are not usually experienced, besides in dreams or during religious exaltation.**"[7] Psychedelics are probably the only substance that can uncover the poets and philosophers that are buried deep down in medical professionals!

However, these long-standing Indigenous health technologies have been subject to **centuries of aggressive suppression,** first through colonization and the Inquisition of the Americas, and later by the US-led "war on drugs" that was launched by President Nixon in 1970.

The motives behind Nixon's campaign are, to this day, disputed (and likely to have been solely political). In any case, its **impacts on the criminalization of marginalized communities are far-reaching and have had a tremendous negative impact.** In the United States, drug offenses are the leading cause of arrest with more than one million people arrested in 2020, which included 350,000 people arrested on marijuana charges. Every ninety seconds on average, someone is arrested for a marijuana offense. Black people make up 24 percent of people arrested for marijuana-related offenses, despite making up just 13 percent of the US population, and despite the fact that Black and White people use and sell drugs at similar rates.[8] To not only avoid more damage but also to benefit from the positive effects psychedelics have to offer, we need to destigmatize, decriminalize and legalize their use.

3) DIFFERENT TYPES OF PSYCHEDELICS

The "classic" psychedelics, the psychedelics with the largest scientific and cultural influence, are **Psilocybin, Ketamine, LSD, MDMA, and DMT**. Many more exist, and for the purpose of this book I will focus on the "classics," for the purpose of healing.[9] Considering that psilocybin is the substance I have been using and recommending, I will start with a deeper dive on this specific medicine.

a) Psilocybin

I. Definition

Psilocybin, commonly referred to as magic mushrooms, is **a natural psychedelic** found in more than two hundred species of fungi. One interesting fact is that, in itself, psilocybin is biologically inactive, but the body converts it rapidly into psilocin which has mind-altering effects. Prehistoric murals in Spain and Algeria imply that psilocybin mushrooms were used by humans long before any medical records and legal frameworks existed. There is literally nothing new under the sun![10]

In the early sixties, when psychedelics were widely researched and prescribed, Timothy Leary and Richard Alpert, then faculty at Harvard University, created the Harvard Psilocybin Project, and found that **the intensity and duration of the effects of psilocybin depended on the species of mushrooms, the dosage, individual physiology, as well as the set and setting.**[11]

The effects of psilocybin mushrooms can include **euphoria, visual and mental hallucinations, changes in perception, a distorted sense of time, and perceived spiritual experiences**. It can also cause adverse reactions such as **nausea and panic attacks.**

Psilocybin works by **activating serotonin receptors**, most often found in the prefrontal cortex. This part of the brain affects mood, cognition, and perception. Hallucinogens also work in other regions of the brain that regulate arousal and panic responses.[12]

II. Usage

For healing purposes psilocybin is traditionally used in the context of a trip meaning individuals take three to five grams of magic mushrooms, often in the company of shamans after setting an intention on what they would like to accomplish during the journey. **A shaman** is someone who **helps others heal by illuminating what is unknown in their being.** Thus, a shaman guides others through altered states of consciousness with the intention of healing. A psychedelic-based journey would be a perfect example of an altered state of consciousness. There has been a long tradition of such trips and shamanism in indigenous cultures across the globe.

Setting a healing intention and working with shamans are the main differences between a healing journey and a recreational trip.

The intentions can be as varied as the individuals who create them. **My intention** during my first psilocybin journey, powered by five grams of golden emperor mushrooms, was to **free myself from blocks, limitations, and negativity**. The experience for me was very physically, emotionally, and mentally intense. During this trip, there was no place for me to hide from my repressed thoughts and feelings, the proverbial cat was out of the bag; dealing with my brother's mortality and my own was pretty awful. But I came back better on the other side. My deep self-loathing was also very present during this journey and it became obvious to me that I was deeply wounded, way more than I could have ever imagined. Beautiful insights, images, and thoughts also came to me. Many people talk about revelations during these journeys. I have to say that my beliefs were already pretty out there, so the idea that "Everything you can imagine is real" didn't strike me as it might have struck many, considering that I already believed that!

My second journey, a couple of days later, was much milder. My intention had been to **amplify the good**, so the trip unfolded accordingly! I also ingested "only" three grams of golden teacher mushrooms, a smaller quantity and a milder strain than during my first trip.

These trips have been a fabulous experience, a combination of healing and transcendental journeys. **My personal psychedelic program revolves around microdosing psilocybin all year round and a plant-medicine ceremony involving larger dose and shamanic guidance every eighteen months.**

III. Benefits

Scientific studies and anecdotal data abound when it comes to the benefits of psilocybin for healing. Most often, these studies are focused on larger doses than microdosing would recommend.

When it comes to scientific and medical research, it is important to note **that science is not yet advanced enough to fully understand the impacts of psychedelics on the mind (conscious and unconscious), the body, the emotions, and their interconnectedness.** The brain is still a great mystery to us and it may take decades before our medical professionals are capable of fully taking in the benefits of psilocybin.

By the same token, this limited knowledge when it comes to our mind and brain explains why mental health has always taken a back seat to physical health. **The astonishing level of complexity of our brains, and of the mind-body connection, has been detrimental to its own research and understanding.**

Nonetheless, a tremendous number of studies have been in motion over the last few years, which have resulted in drastic changes of perspective when it comes to the benefits of psychedelics on mental health. To acknowledge psilocybin **impressive safety record and potential for treating depression more effectively than existing therapies**, the Food and Drug Administration declared the substance a breakthrough therapy in 2018 and 2019 for treating drug-resistant depression and major depressive disorder.[13]

In addition, the United States Department of Veterans Affairs has launched clinical trials to study the effectiveness of psychedelic drugs including MDMA and psilocybin as a treatment for **military veterans with post-traumatic stress disorder, addiction, and other serious mental health issues.**[14]

Lawmakers of all stripes are hard at work in the Western hemisphere to **grant access to these new forms of medicines in answer to the ever-growing mental health crisis**. Veterans and first-responders are front and center in the minds of politicians, paving the way for the general population to experience and benefit from these new treatments.

The delivery models for psilocybin-based medicines will likely come from multiple avenues—**from the traditional healthcare system, to religious organizations, to self-administration.**

I believe there is a time and place for all of these modes of healing, even if I personally prefer giving more power and control to the patient via the self-management of microdosing psilocybin. I do recognize, however, than in certain circumstances, such as severe afflictions, significant oversight will be beneficial to the individual. However, this should not be the default mode. I microdose psilocybin, safely, responsibly, and strategically like all of the people I advise. We don't need to report to an authority figure to do so. Combining the heavy medicalized disease-focused approach of the West, with the natural and health-centered approach of the East, is, from my perspective, the best way to go. If I need a mammogram, I am happy to go see my doctor to do so. Nonetheless, I don't need someone involved in my every decision when it comes to my personal health, at the same time taking away my personal power.

One of the great benefits of psilocybin is to create more emotional and mental freedom, thus liberating oneself from the omnipresent shackles of authority, conditioning, norms, and rules.

By alleviating mental illnesses such as depression, addiction, PTSD, and anxiety, psilocybin can (and hopefully will) revolutionize the world and the way we experience it. Imagine entire cities liberated from addiction and their corollaries, or companies freed from anxiety. What new innovative ideas could blossom on such fertile fields!

In addition, psilocybin has been known to **improve performance by increasing creativity, focus, and attention.**

If all that was not enough, **improved awareness, compassion, as well as connection with oneself and others** have been witnessed in consumers of psilocybin. I can definitely see how these qualities could upgrade our lives at home, at work, and in society in general.

The combination of mental health with improved abilities and sense of awareness could create a new era for humanity.

What lives would you lead if you were mentally healthy, performant, and connected? What life would we lead if the majority of us were mentally healthy, performant, and connected?

This can seem too good to be true, but every day scientific studies are bringing more data supporting this potential scenario. Actually, centuries of anecdotal evidence from across the globe have already done so, but unfortunately their voices have been smothered. Hopefully you are hearing them today and thinking "Sign me up and please sign everyone else I come into contact with!"

Despite a legal status that is at best murky in most North-American jurisdictions, I took it upon myself to not only **use psychedelics with the intent of bettering myself and others,** but also to **publicly advocate for it.**

I refuse to wait ten, twelve, or fifteen years to be "allowed" to make the most of my life, to achieve my potential and to get *more*, just because the scientific and healthcare communities are timid (and riddled with conflicts of interest). This is it for me. I hope you will also consider a leap of faith for your benefits, the benefits of your family, friends, and society at large.

I am not alone in wishing the betterment of humanity; **Sergey Brin, co-founder of Google, is known to enjoy magic mushrooms**. He is part of a larger trend of technology entrepreneurs who hope that **psychedelics will expand minds, enhance lives, and produce business breakthroughs.**[15]

> **I was blind, but now I see.**
> **John 9:25**

IV. Risks

As with any substance entering your body and mind, there are potential risks associated, even drinking too much water can be dangerous, deadly even.

Psilocybin and psychedelics in general are **not recommended for pregnant or breast-feeding women, minors**, people with certain conditions, such as **personality disorders and schizophrenia**. Some **pre-existing conditions**, like heart and liver disease, increase the chance of negative side effects.[16]

I want to put some **context around the risks linked with the use of psychedelics that have been shouted from the rooftops for decades now**.

First, **many claims around psychedelics and their potential risks contain disinformation**. You have likely heard the story claiming that six college students took LSD and went blind. Back in the 60s, State Commissioner for the Blind, Norman Yoder, fabricated this tale out of thin air, just because he didn't like the counter-culture symbol that LSD was. Newspapers picked it up without fact-checking anything. Here we are, sixty years later, and people still have this story in the back of their minds, despite absolutely no truth to it whatsoever.[17]

Second, **there are many things that we know are not safe in the long run: alcohol, cigarettes, and sugary food**. And I would argue that gambling, over-consuming, and sedentary lifestyles are also risky and unhealthy behaviors. But they are all legal and widely accessible. They are also widely socially acceptable, and actually considered to be "cool" when it comes to alcohol. Everyone knows that drinking alcohol, smoking, and mindless eating will bring a long list of health challenges from depression and anxiety to diabetes and cancer. Nevertheless, we are pretty much all doing it to some degree or another. You might say, "Yes, but it is different, they are legal." But should they be? If you believe they should be because you are a responsible adult in charge of your choices (and I am with you on this one), why then would access to psilocybin be any different while it actually has proven benefits and no proven harm so far? If you believe that psilocybin is bad (again, despite the proven benefits and no proven harm), then to be consistent, shouldn't alcohol, cigarettes, and fatty or sugary foods be illegal too?

As you can imagine, **no government will ever go in the direction of ruling out unhealthy products such as alcohol and cigarettes**. Not only is there way too much money and power at play, but you can be sure that there will be more people protesting on the streets than in France when reforming pensions (or to defend democracy in developed countries for that matter).

If this conundrum is getting your critical thinking going, **have a look at the side effects of Prozac (aka Fluoxetine) and ask yourself: does it feel safe now and in the long run**? Even with a doctor prescription and "oversight," I have to say, they got me at decreased sex drive, nervousness, anxiety, difficulty sleeping, and uncontrollable shaking! Who would not want to trade depression for anxiety and impotence? Forty million people take

Prozac worldwide. Despite the fact that, **in 2008, a major scientific review concluded that Prozac does not work, nor do similar drugs in the same class.**[18] Why, then, is it still prescribed despite a long list of side-effects and no conclusive evidence of efficiency? I will leave it to you to make your own conclusions!

Similarly, **the entire world, or almost, got vaccinated multiple times over the past three years and we have, obviously, no clue about the long-term effects of the various shots we all received**. To make an astrology parallel, I am a Moderna Sun AstraZeneca Moon with Pfizer rising. This combination seems like a ticking time bomb.

So if your biggest fear regarding microdosing psilocybin is "will it be harmful in the long run?" (despite all the scientific evidence gathered so far), **ask yourself if this is where your attention should go**—toward a totally unsubstantiated "maybe," versus a certain "yes" when it comes to alcohol, cigarettes, food, Prozac, and potentially the Covid vaccine.

Are our trust and fear of authority figures blinding us? And when I say "our" I mean Gen X, as it seems to me that younger generations are way more apt at questioning the legitimacy of the status quo. **We all know that decisions are made for money and power, not for the well-being of citizens; however, we still think and act as if we were living under the rules of servant leaders, while we are not even governed by paternalistic leaders.**

I am a responsible adult, and in view of the systemic (and systematic) inconsistencies of the healthcare system due to the special interests ruling the industry which prevents the best decisions to be made for the citizens, **I don't see why I would have to subjugate myself to any rules preventing me from making the best decisions for my own health.** Call it civil disobedience.

Others have crossed the Rubicon from passive to active resistance; on July 27th, 2022, patients suffering from cancer, depression, cluster headaches, and other serious health concerns, as well as one healthcare practitioner, sued Canada's federal government. In the lawsuit, they asserted a **constitutional right to medicinal "magic mushroom" access** rooted in s. 7 of Canada's constitutional Charter of Rights and Freedoms. Why the Canadian government is spending taxpayer dollars to fight this case is the billion dollar question.

b) Ketamine

Ketamine is well-known for being an anesthetic, however, doctors sometimes prescribe it for "off-label" uses, such as depression, anxiety, and PTSD.[19] Indeed, over the last few years, **growing research has found that the medicine also works for treatment-resistant depression in some people**, which led the FDA to approve a version called esketamine, or Spravato, in 2019. It's an inhaled treatment that must be administered at a doctor's office, and it is approved only for people for whom other treatments have failed.[20]

Accordingly, you may have noticed ketamine clinics popping up across North America. These clinics offer the medicine off-label as either an infusion or an injection for a wide variety of mental health problems. "Off label" use means the drug hasn't been specifically approved for those conditions.

At this point, ketamine treatments, also known as ketamine-assisted therapy, include ketamine and more or less extensive counselling, and in some cases, integration. The high costs of these treatments and the lack of coverage by health insurers make them accessible only to the lucky few who can afford them.

Entrepreneurs, investors, and executives have reported using Ketamine. Elon Musk, founder of Tesla, microdoses ketamine for depression.[21]

c) LSD

LSD (lysergic acid diethylamide) was originally derived from "ergot," a fungus that grows on rye and other grains.[22]

In its pure state, LSD is a white, odorless crystalline substance. However, **LSD is so potent that an effective dose of the pure drug is so small, it's virtually invisible.** As a result, it's usually diluted with other materials.[23]

Similarly to other psychedelics, when small doses are taken, LSD can produce **mild changes in perception, mood, and thought, while larger doses may produce visual hallucinations and distortions of space and time.**

In the 1950s, 60s, and 70s, intellectuals such as Aldous Huxley, artists such as The Beatles, and entrepreneurs such as Steve Jobs used (and abused) LSD (also commonly called acid) to **boost their creativity and have mystical experiences.**

> **"Taking LSD was a profound experience, one of the most important things in my life. LSD shows you that there's another side to the coin."**
> **–Steve Jobs**

In one notable clinical study in 1963, patients at a Veterans Affairs clinic in Kansas **took LSD to treat alcoholism.**

Today, like with other psychedelics, LSD is seeing **a resurgence in popularity** both in small (microdosing) and large (macrodosing) amounts.

Clinical trials are ongoing regarding the efficiency of LSD to alleviate mental illnesses such as anxiety.[24]

d) MDMA

MDMA stands for methyl enediox-methamphetamine; it is commonly known as ecstasy or molly. It is a synthetic substance that produces **an energizing effect, distortions in time and perception, and enhanced enjoyment from sensory experiences.** It has also been described as an entactogen—a drug that can **increase self-awareness and empathy.**[25]

In 2017, the US Food and Drug Administration (FDA) granted Breakthrough Therapy Designation to MDMA for the treatment of **post-traumatic stress disorder (PTSD)**. This label is given to new drugs when preliminary studies suggest they would be more effective than standard treatments for serious conditions.

This designation opened the door to researchers to perform new clinical trials. The first of these new psychedelic trials, at a Veterans Affairs clinic in California, aims to treat combat veterans with post-traumatic stress disorder with MDMA.[26] Used in combination with psychotherapy, the preliminary results of the ongoing studies are nothing short of promising.

Once best known as a party drug, MDMA, alongside other psychedelics, is now shaking up psychiatry.

e) DMT

N, N-dimethyltryptamine (DMT) is a hallucinogenic tryptamine drug that naturally occurs in many plant species and can also be made in a laboratory. DMT is a strong but relatively short-acting psychedelic compound that is rapidly metabolized by the body. It produces **short but intense psychedelic "trips" that can induce hallucinations while also affecting the user's thinking, mood, and sense of time**. Various cultures use DMT for its consciousness-altering properties in spiritual rituals.

A Phase IIa clinical trial of DMT for **the treatment of major depressive disorder** (MDD) has announced **positive preliminary findings** from the trial's six-month data. The data suggests that some patients with MDD may benefit from treatment with the short-acting psychedelic compound alongside supportive therapy.[27]

• • • • •

The psychedelics mentioned above have **great variability when it comes to their potency**. A microdose of LSD will be much smaller in size and weight than a microdose of psilocybin. The rule of thumb for a **microdose is five to ten percent of a full dose**.

At this point, it **is difficult to say which psychedelics will fare "better" for patients' mental health**. Consumers tend to favour natural to synthetic drugs, a phenomenon known as the **"natural preference."** Current research shows that while consumers have a general preference for natural drugs over synthetic drugs, this preference is stronger when the goal is to treat psychological rather than physical conditions. Consumers are indeed more concerned about their true selves being altered when treating psychological conditions, and they perceive natural drugs to be less likely than synthetic drugs to affect their true selves.[28] **Accordingly, we can extrapolate that psilocybin would likely be the preferred choice for the average patient.**

Psychedelics can be used in microdose or in macrodose. When it comes to macrodosing, the assistance of experts is highly recommended. When preparing for a macrodose journey, there is a big difference to keep in mind between a guide—someone who will support the patient through their consciousness-altering experience—and a sitter—someone who will just insure that the patient is fine during the journey.

Whether micro or macrodosing, **the jury is still out regarding the value of combining therapy and psychedelics.** For many, psychedelics can lead to internal experiences that are better lived than shared and dissected with a third party. I tend to agree with this point of view for a macrodose journey. In the context of microdosing though, the combination of alternative modalities, such as the ones presented in The Microdose Diet, is a significant plus. Considering that the intensity and time span are widely different between macrodosing (a few intense hours) and microdosing (mild sensations for weeks, months, or years) it makes sense that the approach diverges significantly too.

If, from a purely scientific perspective, many questions are still outstanding, anecdotal facts collected for centuries and early stage data from recent studies point toward **a net positive outcome when it comes to the use of psychedelics for healing.** In the 1950s and 1960s, many scientists regarded psychedelics as a potentially revolutionary tool in the treatment of addiction and other psychiatric conditions.

In the last ten years, psychedelics have strongly reemerged as medicines with the potential to address mental illness and enhance well-being among largely non-Indigenous communities. The current studies are happening amid a global rethinking of the dangers and potential benefits of substances that were outlawed and demonized during the presidencies of Lyndon B. Johnson and Richard M. Nixon. According to historians, both leaders were concerned that psychedelic drugs were fueling opposition to the war in Vietnam War and other government activities, driving their decisions to crack down on psychedelic research and usage.

Today, these different substances are currently being researched in multiple capacities, offering the potential for a world with stronger mental health.

Spot the gaslighting and see through the bullshit.

Key Takeaways – Chapter 2

- Psychedelics can either be **plant-based or chemically-produced**. The **"classic"** psychedelics, the psychedelics with the largest scientific and cultural influence, are **Psilocybin, Ketamine, LSD, MDMA, and DMT**.
- Psychedelics are powerful **psychoactive substances**, meaning they **affect how the brain works and cause changes in mood, awareness, thoughts, feelings, or behavior.**
- They are generally considered **physiologically safe** and **do not lead to dependence or addiction.**
- **Psychedelics give us the ability to take advantage of a concept called neuroplasticity**, the fact that our brains are ever-changing in response to stimuli. Put very simply, this means that **it really is possible to rewire our brains.**
- They have a long history of use, but have been subjected to **centuries of aggressive suppression.**
- Scientific studies and anecdotal data abound when it comes to the **benefits of psychedelics for healing**. One of these benefits is to create **more emotional and mental freedom.** They also have been known to **improve performance by increasing creativity, focus, and attention**. In addition, **improved awareness and compassion as well as connection with oneself** and others have been witnessed.
- To acknowledge psilocybin **impressive safety record and potential for treating depression more effectively than existing therapies**, the Food and Drug Administration designated psilocybin a breakthrough therapy in 2018 and 2019 for treating drug-resistant depression and major depressive disorder.

- The US Department of Veterans Affairs has launched clinical trials to study the effectiveness of psychedelic drugs as treatment for **military veterans with post-traumatic stress disorder, addiction, and other serious mental health issues.**
- Psychedelics are **not recommended for pregnant or breast-feeding women, minors**, or people with certain conditions, such as **personality disorders and schizophrenia.** Some **pre-existing conditions**, like heart and liver disease, increase the chance of negative side-effects.
- Psychedelics can be taken as a **microdose** or as a **macrodose**, creating widely different experiences and results. They have **great variability when it comes to their potency.**
- A large trend of technology entrepreneurs, such as Sergey Brin, co-founder of Google, hope that **psychedelics will expand minds, enhance lives, and produce business breakthroughs.**

Chapter 3

From the Psychedelic Renaissance to the Psychedelic Gentrification

The term Psychedelic Renaissance has been used since 2014 in reference to the **resurgence of interest from the medical and scientific communities into psychedelics**, particularly for therapeutic purposes and with regard to mental health.

The impetus for this renaissance is mainly found in the increase in mental health issues and the inability of our current systems (medical, judicial, societal) to address them. Whether the mental health crisis finds its sources in social media, human disconnection, nutrition, sedentary lifestyles, discrimination, trauma, or genetics, that's not the topic of this book. The point is that we are living in a watershed movement when it comes to the human and financial costs of mental illness.

In 2019, the World Health Organization reported that one in every eight people, or close to **one billion people around the world, were living with a mental disorder, with anxiety and depressive disorders being the most common.** In 2020, the number of people living with anxiety and depressive disorders rose significantly because of the COVID-19 pandemic. Initial estimates show a **26 percent and 28 percent increase respectively for anxiety and major depressive disorders in just one year.**[29]

No matter how staggering these numbers are, **I believe they are grossly under representing the extent of the mental health crisis.**

First, it is extremely difficult to assess what represents a mental health challenge. This explains why we have seen **so little focus on mental health investments** from the healthcare industry in the past. How do you prove one's mental health was impaired, that it has improved, and that your treatment is effective? It is not like a broken leg or a cancer with very demonstrable symptoms and results. When healthcare companies have to choose where to allocate their capital for researching new treatments, they do so on the basis of business cases; size of the addressable market; pricing of the new treatments; probability of success; timelines; and cost of the research. Rationally so, they will go in the direction that will maximize their profits (not societal well-being, in case you had any doubt about their intentions) and minimize the risks; shareholders rule! If it is difficult to prove that there was a problem in the first place and that the treatment made it better, companies will not take the financial risks to invest in the research, and who could blame them. This is how capitalism works.

Second, unless the mental illness is very acute, it is extremely difficult to diagnose who is suffering. Most people live with poor mental health and don't even know it. From a lack of information to stigma, there are many reasons for this deficiency of self-assessment. I was the prime example of this; I had no idea that I was suffering from PTSD, anxiety, and depression. Not knowing what these diseases stood for and being totally oblivious to the fact that my "normal state" was far from optimal, as it was the only state I knew, I would have ranked (and did rank) my mental health as excellent. And I am far from being alone in that illusion; people in their seventies and eighties are now coming out of the woodwork, realizing that they probably have had mental illnesses such as depression, anxiety, or PTSD their entire lives.

Third, the brain is still a mystery for the medical field. That might be the most important reason why mental health has been left aside and illnesses have been underestimated for so long. In a 2019 interview, Christof Koch, Ph.D., Chief Scientist and President of the Allen Institute for Brain Science, was asked how close we were to understanding our own brains. His answer was pretty candid and enlightening: **"We don't even understand the brain of a worm."**[30] This immense lack of knowledge is one of the reasons I always find it interesting when I am asked what the scientific and medical communities think about microdosing psilocybin. To start, the thoughts of these communities are all over the place and, based on their own a priori, the feedback will be widely different. Also, well-funded studies can prove or disprove anything, climate change being a prime example of this. Finally, based on the numerous misdiagnosis and medical mistakes that happen every day, even for common ailments, I believe it is wise to form our own informed opinions. In the next thirty to fifty years, much more will be known regarding our brains and the impact of mind-altering substances, not least of all because of the support of artificial intelligence. Today, though, we are still in the infancy of understanding not only psychedelics but also the brain (and I am not even referring to our mind and spirit).

When it comes to mental illness, humanity is facing a reckoning that no number can accurately represent. This offers tremendous opportunities in the way we address mental health challenges. **The combination of psychotherapy and anti-depressants has been showing its limit in helping people get back to their optimal level of mental health.** It is true that the drugs prescribed liberally by the medical apparatus never aimed at curing the illness, but rather, merely relieving the symptoms. I totally believe in using a crutch to get past difficult moments that one will inevitably face in their lives. However, alleviating symptoms in the long run instead of addressing the root causes is not sustainable for the patient. It is undoubtedly profitable though for the pharmaceutical companies who create tremendous recurring revenues and valuation for themselves; yes, they are for-profit organizations not NGOs working for the greater good of humanity. Regarding psychotherapy, as brilliantly demonstrated by Gabor Maté in his book *The Myth of Normal* and numerous talks associated, therapy is far from being the panacea.[31] When one can find a therapist, the question of their competency remains.

Hence the situation we are finding ourselves in, which is mainly the reason behind the Psychedelic Renaissance; **more mental illnesses are diagnosed and no solid treatments to cure the patients exist.**

In addition, and above and beyond the medical and humanitarian aspects of the mental health problem, this state of affairs has very **large economic implications**. Lost productivity as a result of two of the most common mental disorders—anxiety and depression—costs the global economy one trillion dollars each year. Poor mental health was estimated to cost the world economy approximately **two to five trillion dollars per year** in poor health and reduced productivity in 2010, a cost projected to **rise to six trillion by 2030.**[32] These numbers don't even take into consideration the costs of the drugs and health practitioners.

On the bright side, for our entrepreneurial and savvy investor readers, this means that **there are huge business opportunities.**

All of this put together brought us the Psychedelic Renaissance. Almost ten years later, I believe we are now **past the point of the Renaissance and are in full Gentrification mode.** I see five main signs that we have now entered what I call the **Psychedelic Gentrification.**

1) MAINSTREAM CONSUMERS AND DAILY USAGES

Psychedelics that were used in the past in large quantities for "trips" by hippies are **now used daily in microdoses by CEOs, VCs, Moms, and every day people for performance, mental wellness, happiness, and personal transformation.**

In an interview in *The Wall Street Journal* in 2023, Spencer Shulem, CEO of BuildBetter.ai, said he uses LSD about every three months because it increases focus and helps him think more creatively. From his perspective, "[Investors] don't want a normal person, a normal company. They want something extraordinary. You're not born extraordinary."[33]

In parallel, **hundreds of veterans have been traveling to psychedelic retreat centers abroad.** Many have become advocates for expanding access to hallucinogens in their home countries.

The images of long-haired, free-spirited guys zoned out on a beach somewhere are definitely a thing of the past.

2) SURGES IN VISIBILITY

Answering to the **growing interest from millions**, world-class publications such as *The Economist, The Wall Street Journal, Financial Times,* and *The Washington Post,* have been widely reporting on the progress psychedelics have made in the last few years—all after decades of psychedelics being shunned by the mainstream media.

Even more telling, **lifestyle magazines have been tripping over themselves to cover the advance of psychedelics** by showcasing stories of women (usually Moms) who have seen their lives transformed thanks to psychedelics—mostly by microdosing psilocybin.

3) LEGAL FRAMEWORK IN RAPID MOTION

After fifty years of unfair stigmatization, courtesy of the Nixon administration, the legal establishment, never one to move fast, has surprised players all around the world with weekly announcements around **legalization, decriminalization, and reclassification of psychedelics**.

In the United States, bipartisan legislations have been popping up across the country, including in mostly conservative areas. Understanding that psychedelics is a **public health topic**, not a political one, more and more elected officials on both sides of the aisle are taking a supportive stance.

Most recently, Australia has announced that it will recognize **psilocybin and MDMA as medicines** that can be used to help those who suffer with post-traumatic stress disorder and depression.

In Canada, while still officially illegal, magic mushroom **dispensaries have begun to pop up across the country**, in a move not dissimilar to what we have witnessed with Cannabis pre-legalization.

4) SCIENTIFIC STUDIES ON STEROIDS

It was only in 2018 that the **US Food and Drug Administration** named psilocybin a "breakthrough therapy" in the treatment of severe depression, and since then, a tidal wave of studies have begun, bringing more encouraging data to the conversation.

Across the globe, scientists have been actively engaged in an exponential number of clinical trials with organizations such as the US and Canadian Department of Veterans Affairs that have been **enthusiastically testing the use of psychedelics to support the mental health of their members**.

5) BUSINESS CREATION AND INCREASED CAPITAL ALLOCATION

The market for psychedelics is projected to grow **from two billion in 2020 to close to eleven billion dollars by 2027**; accordingly, savvy investors and businesspeople have been busy developing new companies and investment funds to capture the profits.

Brand name investors such as **Christian Angermayer, Tim Ferriss, and Peter Thiel** have been active in the space alongside institutional investors such as **LongeVC, Tabula Rasa Ventures, JLS Fund, Noetic Psychedelic Fund, and The Conscious Fund**.

There are already **more than fifty publicly traded companies** related to the development and administration of psychedelic-like drugs in the United States alone.

6) WHAT DOES IT MEAN FOR YOU?

There may still be a stigma today, but it's clear that **the wheels of a cultural revolution around the use of psychedelics have already begun to turn.**

There are two main reasons you should care about the Psychedelic Gentrification;

a) Increasing Your Well-Being

As more and more studies have been demonstrating, psychedelics have the ability to **significantly improve your mood, mindset, and overall level of happiness**. I am personally delighted to be able to benefit from this general uplevelling now, versus in five years, and would have loved to have benefited from it five or ten years ago.

b) Riding The Biggest Wave Early

I like to be early on trends. It was the case for me with Fintech and now it is the case with psychedelics. I pivoted all of my activities toward psychedelics, not only because I am a believer (which, let's be honest, was the main initial reason), but also because **I recognize the value of riding the biggest wave early**. Psychedelics are not a wave; they are a tsunami and I want to be ideally positioned to capitalize from the disruption.

Similarly, you have the opportunity to **benefit from the Psychedelic Gentrification now** for your own **personal transformation**, as well as for **your investments and career.**

The time is now, you have been warned!

How to improve the healthcare system with alternative medicines.

Key Takeaways - Chapter 3

- **The Psychedelic Renaissance** is the resurgence of interest from the medical and scientific communities into psychedelics.
- The impetus for this renaissance is mainly found in **the increase in mental health issues** and the **inability of our current system** (medical, judicial, societal) **to address them.**
- In 2019, even pre-Covid, close to **one billion people around the world were living with a mental disorder, with anxiety and depressive disorders being the most common.**
- We are past the point of the Renaissance and are now in **full Gentrification mode.**
- Poor mental health was estimated to cost the world economy approximately **two to five trillion dollars per year** in poor health and reduced productivity in 2010, a cost projected to **rise to six trillion by 2030.**
- Five signs that we have now entered what I call the **Psychedelic Gentrification: Mainstream Consumers and Daily Usages; Surges in Visibility; Legal Framework in Rapid Motion; Scientific Studies on Steroids; Business Creation; and Increased Capital Allocation.**
- The wheels of a cultural revolution around the use of psychedelics have **already begun to turn.**
- What does it mean for you? **1) Increasing your well-being; 2) Riding the biggest wave early.**
- You have the opportunity to **benefit from the Psychedelic Gentrification now** for your own **personal transformation**, as well as for **your investments and career.**

Chapter 4

Microdosing Psilocybin 101

This chapter will give you a nice overview of **what it means to microdose psilocybin**. Based on your location, this might be a legal option for you or not. I will not make recommendations or pass judgment on your choice. This decision is one you have to make on your own. You know by now that exercising critical thinking and questioning everything are the foundations of this book. Regardless of your decision, you can always revisit it later based on your personal situation, comfort level, and legislation progress.

1) WHAT IS MICRODOSING?

Imagine eating one piece of sushi. You probably wouldn't feel much different, right? But what if you ate twenty or thirty pieces? You'd likely be quite sick (or at least extremely full).

In very general terms, this is the difference in the amount of psilocybin needed for microdosing versus "tripping." **Microdosing is like eating one piece of sushi, while macrodosing is like eating an entire sampler platter**. There is also mesodosing, which is somewhere in between. Mesodosing and macrodosing can be useful in certain situations, but they are emphatically *not* part of the 90 Day Microdose Diet. They can provoke intense experiences that should only be attempted in a controlled environment. They also have very different aims.

Microdosing, on the other hand, fits into a daily routine, and the physical effects—if they're noticeable at all—**will be less intense than the jolt you get after your morning cup of coffee**. It's only over time that you will start to notice a difference. It should be noted that while psychedelics have been used for thousands of years, scientific research in the field is still blossoming. Findings have so far been very positive, and **what we will know in fifty years might be even more exciting than what we know today**.

2) WHAT IS THE BEST WAY TO MICRODOSE?

Similarly to the initial process doctors and patients undergo with the introduction of any prescribed drug, a new microdosing regimen involves an element of experimentation. Fortunately, **psilocybin comes with a lot of possibility for personalization**; there are many components you can adjust until you find out what suits you best.

a) Type Of Mushroom

Magic mushrooms exist in all shapes and sizes, with varying potency. The one commonality is psilocybin, the main hallucinogenic found within all magic mushrooms. The most common form of magic mushroom is arguably the psilocybe cubensis. Within this species, **the golden teacher is by far my favorite mushroom as I consider it the microdosing beginners' darling**. Many others are available for microdosers, such as the Penis Envy (which, from my perspective, could benefit from a rebrand) or the B+, to only name the most common.

b) Frequency

If you've ever taken antibiotics (or really any prescription drug), you've probably had it drilled into your head that you need to **be diligent about taking the medicine at the same time each day and finishing the entire regimen**. You can shift that mentality when taking psilocybin. You certainly don't need to take it every day, and you also don't need to commit for the rest of your life. In fact, there are three schools of thought around frequency of consumption. Some people take it each weekday but not on the weekends. Others take it every other day. Another option is every third day. The 90 Day Microdose Diet presented in section 2 of this book, as well as in the online course available at themicrodosediet.com, will guide you through the recommended frequency as you're just getting started.

c) Dosage

Starting with 100 mg of psilocybin is a great rule of thumb. It's easy to remember and it's a good amount for most people. You might prefer to experiment with a higher dosage (e.g. 150 mg) to get a feel for the physical effects, then you can decrease over time. The 90 Day Microdose Diet will be your guide here as well.

d) Forms

Psilocybin comes in three main forms: edibles, caps, and dry mushrooms. Each one is unique, and different people have their own preferences. In general, caps are easiest because they're already measured for the desired dose and there are options for including adaptogenic mushrooms that provide additional benefits, such as stress reduction, improved mental clarity and increased energy. Edibles are my preference when making micro adjustments to the dosage, because it's simple to quickly cut off a different amount each day. Dry mushrooms are the most "back to basics" approach but can be difficult for beginners because they require a very precise scale to measure the exact amount. **The main advantage of using dry mushrooms is the ability to grow the mushrooms at home, guaranteeing a constant quality supply and usually benefiting from a friendlier legal framework.**

e) Timing

I generally advise taking psilocybin first thing in the morning to ensure a consistant and optimal experience. An empty stomach is best, but it's also fine to take it with food if it makes you feel nauseated. I believe that sticking to the same mushrooms, dosage, and frequency for a period of at least three weeks will allow for enough data points to be collected before any adjustment should be considered.

f) Supply

Depending on your geography, you will be able to source quality psilocybin more or less easily. Quality level is important, as well as constancy in effects. Whether you decide to forage, grow your own, or buy off the shelf, **I highly recommend validating the**

quality of your supply. I have actually been collaborating with top notch producers and distributers to provide premium micro-dosing products to my audience. It was never my intention to go in that part of the business, but the need was so obvious that I got sucked in. You can learn more and place your order at themicro-dosediet.com.

3) THE MANY BENEFITS AND LIMITED RISKS OF MICRODOSING PSILOCYBIN

The following are quotes from the movie *Limitless* with Bradley Cooper. They give a great overview of how microdosing has been working for many.

"What was this drug? I couldn't stay messy on it. [...] I wasn't high. I wasn't wired. Just clear. I knew what I needed to do and how to do it."

"All my fear? All my shyness? Gone!"

"A tablet a day and what I could do with my day was limitless."

In alignment to the data points on psilocybin, there have been important shifts across several areas of my life since I started microdosing. Though the exact effects vary for each individual, I generally find that they fall into three key categories:

a) Performance

I have always been a top performer in professional settings, but there is no question that **microdosing has sharpened my focus and expanded my concentration**, as has been the case for most adopters of this regimen. This came to bear fruit when I sat down to write my first book and managed to crank out a forty-thousand-word novel in a mere ten days. Every time I had previously sat down in front of my computer with the same aim, I had struggled with the dreaded writer's block. Microdosing makes me feel

much more creative: new ideas come easily and I am quickly able to **find clarity** on which to pursue. When I get on stage or attend networking events, I am **much more relaxed** than I ever was before microdosing. I can now enjoy these opportunities for social interaction and connection, rather than stressing about my performance or how I will be perceived. **My ability to absorb and remember new information has also greatly improved.** All these benefits have been widely recorded and accepted in the microdosing community.

Unexpectedly, microdosing has also had a **positive impact on my athletic performance.** I am fortunate to have natural athletic abilities, but I had never really thrived in any particular sport. Instead, I let myself be sidelined by a lack of confidence and limiting beliefs like, "I am not good enough to play," "I should not shine too brightly or others might take offense," and "What if I push too hard and get hurt?" **Microdosing has proven to have both physical benefits (increased focus, decreased reaction time, optimized balance) as well as mental ones (elevated confidence, increased flow and fun, minimized performance anxiety).** These benefits are by far not unique to me. According to the Multidisciplinary Association for Psychedelic Studies, "The extreme sports underground have been using psychedelics for more than forty years to increase reflex time to lightning speeds, improve balance to the point of perfection, increase concentration until you experience 'tunnel vision,' and make you impervious to weakness or pain."

b) Mental Wellness

Since I started microdosing, I have a noticeably **more positive outlook and increased zest for life**. Rather than always imagining and preparing for the worst-case scenario, I now go into situations expecting success. This has made a significant difference in my levels of anxiety and stress. I am able to enjoy downtime free of guilt about the outstanding things on my to-do list, which I was never able to do before. **My perspective on what matters and what doesn't has totally shifted.** Overall, I find that I am much **more present in my daily life and the days actually feel longer**. My symptoms of depression are long gone and even challenging to remember. Mental health is actually the area on which most scientific studies and medical trials focus on—**from treating anxiety and stress to depression and PTSD, the results so far have been extremely encouraging.**

c) Consciousness

As you will learn through the 90 Day Microdose Diet, a key component of microdosing is clearing out the existing cobwebs (things like self-doubt, limiting beliefs, and reliance on "the way I've always done it") **to make room for your new limitless potential.** To maximize psilocybin's ability to reprogram the mind, I am guiding readers through a daily short and easy mindfulness practice in combination with their microdosing routine. I have focused on modalities like tapping, visualization, and guided meditation. Through incorporating these practices, I have found that it is much easier and faster to **shift ingrained beliefs and release limitations**, such as scarcity and adversity mindsets that have been life-changing for the protagonists.

Though the benefits are numerous, do I think psilocybin is for everyone? Of course not. Unlike many other drugs, there is no recorded evidence of anyone ever overdosing on mushrooms. Still, you need to be mindful of not overdoing it, unless you are being guided and monitored by professionals. I also want to be clear that you should not consider microdosing if you are someone who struggles with a condition like schizophrenia or if you are pregnant. We all have different bodies, mental health needs, and mindsets. **My results are linked with my own personal situation and a carefully monitored microdosing routine. Similarly, your unique biology, habits, and lifestyle will affect yours.** There is really no "one size fits all" approach for anything in life. I researched microdosing *extensively* before deciding on whether to start incorporating it into my life, and even now I stay very up-to-date on research and news. I suggest that everyone do their own investigation to decide if microdosing is a practice that may fit into their lives. After all, knowledge is power.

As mentioned in The Microdose Diet protocol, I recommend that you keep track of your progress in all areas of your life when you decide to follow a microdosing regimen. **Otherwise, it is too easy to lose track of the state you were in mentally, emotionally, or physically, when you actually started** the program. The tendency to constantly rebaseline or set a "New Normal," is healthy as it generates growth. However, it might impede your ability to accurately assess all the progress that has been made over time.

4) A NOTE ON THE LEGAL STATUS OF PSILOCYBIN MUSHROOMS

Where is it legal today to consume psilocybin mushrooms? That is, of course, the million-dollar question. It's more complicated than you might imagine. As mentioned throughout this book, we are seeing a very rapid evolution of the legislative framework when it comes to psychedelics. **At the time of publication of this book, the legal status of psilocybin would have already seen many changes, probably in the direction of decriminalization**

and legalization. Differences exist based on geography but also based on the type of psychedelics, their usage (health or recreational), who administers them, and who receives them. Each country, state, province, or even municipality, has a different approach when it comes to the decriminalization or legalization of mushrooms.

In the United States, major cities such as Denver, Santa Cruz, and Oakland have decriminalized the use of psilocybin in recent years. In Oregon and Colorado, state legislation is setting precedents regarding the legalization of psilocybin. **In Canada, it is legal to purchase spores and pre-inoculated grow kits** (as they don't contain psilocybin). **Picking mushrooms in nature is also permitted.**

Mainstream media such as *The Economist, The Wall Street Journal, Harper's Bazaar, 60 Minutes,* and the *Today Show* have been covering the Psychedelic Renaissance with great enthusiasm. It is clear that public opinion is shifting, especially as people increasingly understand that **there is an important difference between recreational use and wellness-oriented use of psychedelics.**

Today's movement to decriminalize and legalize psychedelics probably would have happened decades ago if not for Nixon's "war on drugs" that essentially set research back by fifty years. However, **many people still operate under a fallacy that "legal" equals "right" and "illegal" equals "wrong."** Hopefully, more flexibility and clarity will come in the near future as more research is done and both medical professionals and lawmakers begin to understand that not all psychedelics—or psychedelic practices—are created equal.

Work with Peggy for your clients' and employees' events.

Key Takeaways – Chapter 4

- Microdosing is like eating one piece of sushi, while macrodosing is like eating an entire sampler platter. **Five to ten percent of a macrodose is the equivalent of a microdose; based on that, a microdose would be 100 to 250 mg of psilocybin.**
- **Similarly to the initial process doctors and patients undergo with the introduction of any prescribed drug**, a new microdosing regimen involves an element of experimentation.
- Magic mushrooms exist in **all shapes and sizes**, with **varying potency**.
- Be diligent about taking the medicine at **the same time each day and finishing the entire regimen**.
- Starting with **100 mg of psilocybin** is a great rule of thumb.
- Psilocybin comes in three main forms: **edibles, caps, and dry mushrooms**.
- Take psilocybin **first thing in the morning** to ensure a constant and optimal experience.
- I highly recommend to **validate the quality of your supply**.
- The benefits of microdosing psilocybin fall into three categories: **performance, mental wellness, and consciousness**.
- Performance: **sharpened focus, expanded concentration, increased creativity, decreased reaction time, optimized balance, elevated confidence, increased flow, and fun.**
- Mental state: **improved outlook, increased zest for life, heightened presence, minimized anxiety, stress, and depression.**

- Consciousness: **shifted ingrained beliefs and released limitations.**
- Results are linked with **your unique biology, habits, and lifestyle.**

Chapter 5

Psychedelics on Steroids: Combining Best in Class Tools

In Western culture, we're used to having medications readily available to address the symptoms of physical and mental issues. Have a headache? Pop an Advil. Feeling anxious? Take a Xanax.

Though psilocybin isn't a medication, I often find that people have a similar assumption: as long as psilocybin is entering the body, there's nothing else to do in order to experience a change. This may be true to some extent, but I am someone who **wants to not only maximize the effects of the psilocybin, but also have control over *how* my brain is being rewired**. This is why in addition to taking psychedelics, I incorporate other modalities to focus and accelerate the personal transformation you and I seek.

Some of my favorites—which we use throughout the 90 Day Microdose Diet—are tapping, havening, journaling, visualization, and guided meditation.

1) TAPPING AND HAVENING

Also called EFT Tapping (Emotional Freedom Technique), tapping meditation is a modality that has grown in popularity in the Western Hemisphere in the last decade. **Tapping is a powerful stress relief technique, often referred to as an alternative therapy for anxiety, post-traumatic stress disorder (PTSD), and other conditions.**

Tapping uses our physical meridian points to resolve physical and emotional issues. You can think of it as belonging to the same family as acupuncture or acupressure. **By tapping on certain meridian points with your fingertips, you can restore balance in your body and mind to resolve physical and emotional issues.**

How to tap is very straightforward, you use the tip of your fingers to lightly tap on the tapping points (see map below) while following the script along. As you tap, the goal is to mentally "tune in" to the specific issues you wish to address. In this book we are using the Faster EFT Method that streamlines the number of points. The tapping disrupts the signal between the brain and the major organs of the body. This is this signal that triggers the fight, flight, or freeze response. **The disruption of the signal changes the neural pathways in the neocortex of the brain.** Hence, helping you remove the negative charges and reprogram your mind, body and emotions.

In combination with the Faster EFT Method, you will use the Havening Technique which is a self-soothing gesture. The Havening

Technique interrupts and diverts the activity in your amygdala, training it to break the negative associations that have been made in the past. At the end of the scripts, you will then run your hands on your face from top to bottom, very calmly, lightly, and lovingly. **This motion will create a sense of safety and well-being ideal to finish your session.** Throughout The 90 Day Diet, the scripts specifically target the most common and challenging blocks to success, passion and happiness. If you wish to follow along videos you will be able to do so via the online course available at TheMicrodoseDiet.com. Scan the QR code at the end of the chapter to access the online journey. The scripts are the same than those outlined in this book. I lead them and put them in the context of each lesson.

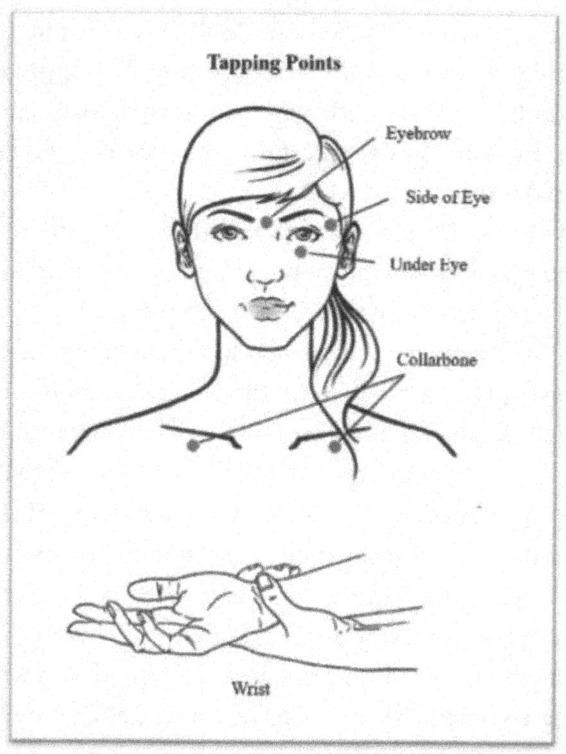

The best way for you to understand the benefits of tapping is to try it. And before you do, know that research has shown that **EFT Tapping lowers cortisol (the stress hormone) by 43 percent.**

If you need more social proof before feeling comfortable tapping with your fingertips on the side of your eyes, collarbone and so on, know that **Tony Robbins is a big supporter of tapping, as is Gabrielle Bernstein.** They both recorded tapping meditations, which are available online. The Havening Method is itself supported by Paul McKenna, a celebrity hypnotist who is a firm believer in its value.

There are myriad ways for you to tap: alongside a coach, by yourself, by following the Tapping Solutions app, YouTube videos, and scripts in books—the list goes on. It's so quick and easy that I have often started tapping as soon as a negative emotion like fear, worry, or frustration starts to bubble.

Tapping can be helpful in multiple situations.

The first is when confronted with the daily irritants of life. You can't sleep, you are worried about paying your bills, you are angry in traffic, you feel agitated, stressed, and so on. Whether you want to tap right away when these uncomfortable feelings arise, or whether you'd rather wait for a more opportune time, you will find great relief when tapping. Tapping on your own will quickly lower the intensity of the feelings and you will be able to see the situation from a less emotionally-triggered perspective.

The second scenario is in the context of limiting beliefs or repeated negative patterns. The example I used regarding my relationship with money would fall into this category. It is likely that long-standing situations have multiple deep roots that will need to be addressed several times via different angles. This is where working with a practitioner (one-on-one or via an online course) will come in handy. And even if you decide to "only" tap alone, you will see benefits.

I tap pretty much every day, whether to deal with the small irritants of life (which I have to admit tend to irritate me less and less!) or to shift my remaining limiting beliefs.

When you tap, don't be surprised by your physical reactions to the tapping (such as yawning, sneezing, or burping), your nervous system is letting go—this is what you want!

2) JOURNALING

Journaling is a very well-known and extremely positive concept when it comes to a healthy mental state. Research suggests that journaling can help us accept rather than judge our mental experiences, resulting in fewer negative emotions in response to stressors.[34]

From reducing anxiety, regulating emotions, breaking away from cycles of obsessive thinking, to increasing awareness, improving perception of events, and speeding up physical healing, journaling offers a treasure trove of advantages.[35]

I love journaling, which might seem obvious for a writer. For me, the simple act of taking a few minutes for myself to put my thoughts, worries, and dreams onto paper not only lightens my heart almost instantly, but it also signals to my conscious and subconscious minds that **I am important enough to allocate time for my own well-being**. Thus improving, even slightly so, my self-generated self-worth.

More prosaically, **journaling gives you a very tangible way to assess your progress**. One can always go back to it when feeling the need for encouragement and additional motivation. The process of writing makes the improvement even more real and permanent. **By giving a target to your brain, it also helps direct your attention toward your success and ultimately your intention.**

When it comes to journaling, handwriting (versus typing) has multiple advantages. First, **handwriting increases neural activity** in certain sections of the brain, which is similar to meditation. The mere act of writing by hand unleashes creativity not easily accessed in any other way. Second, **handwriting sharpens the brain and helps you learn**. Sequential hand movements activate large regions of the brain that are responsible for thinking, language, healing, and working memory.[36] Finally, it **improves critical thinking** by allowing the writer to think more thoroughly about the information recorded.[37]

3) VISUALIZATION

Visualization, also called imagery, uses your imagination to improve your ability to reach your goals. As Einstein notably asserted "**Imagination is more important than knowledge**. For knowledge is limited, whereas imagination embraces the entire world, stimulating progress, giving birth to evolution." With visualization, **we focus the mind on the target we want to reach**. Our brain is like a computer, and we want to install the right software to achieve the optimal outcome. By feeding it the pictures of what we want to achieve, we stimulate it to find creative ways to accomplish our goals.

Visualization has been used for a very long time in sports. From Muhammad Ali to Arnold Schwarzenegger, this technique has had an army of supporters that have used it to reach their goals in and outside of the gymnasium. A study published in *Neuropsychologia* found that **imagining to move certain parts of**

your body almost trains the muscles as much as the actual movement.[38]

Visualization can ultimately help **you gain confidence, enhance performance, boost motivation, decrease anxiety, and reduce stress.**

> **"Anything you can imagine, you can create."**
> **–Oprah Winfrey**

4) GUIDED MEDITATION

Guided meditation refers to the process of meditating under the guidance of a third party; the guidance is essentially an **audible or visual narration.** Because the mind has a tendency to wander, most find it easier to focus and relax when the mind isn't entirely left to its own devices.

Similarly to visualization, guided meditation **harnesses the power of your mind to attain your desired outcomes.** A great combination to tapping, journaling, and visualization (words and pictures) guided meditation allows you to paint a vivid representation of your goals, focusing your brain on making this reality happen. I personally visualize and listen to guided meditation every single day.

You can find fabulous guided meditations on YouTube and Apple Music. I particularly love Alana Fairchild and Joe Dispenza guided meditations. The Tapping Solution application has also started offering recordings of guided meditations, in addition to tapping meditations.

The benefits of guided meditations are multiple: widening imagination, lengthening attention span, strengthening patience, and increasing presence, to only name a few.

• • • • •

These tools will help you uplevel in the context of The Microdose Diet, and can also be used as stand-alone technologies when you have finished your 90 day program and want to **continue to grow**.

Listening to guided meditations (or hypnosis tracks) is the simplest of them all; pop a recording in and go on with your day. I often listen to recordings while getting ready in the morning. Combining visualization to meditation is also a very efficient and easy way to move toward your desired outcomes. Journaling is one of the best ways to process your thoughts and evolve your thinking. It might take you only five minutes to find relief or creative solutions. Tapping can be done pretty much anywhere, or anytime, especially when using the hand's acupressure points—it's definitely more discreet than the head's acupressure points. **Your commute (assuming you are using public transportation!) is an ideal time to use these tools.** Going back to the office might be a good idea after all!

Learn more about The Microdose Diet online journey.

Key Takeaways - Chapter 5

- Tapping, journaling, visualization, and guided meditations are fabulous tools to **maximize the effects of the psilocybin**, and have control over **how your brain is being rewired.**
- **Tapping is a powerful stress relief technique**, often referred to as an alternative therapy for anxiety, post-traumatic stress disorder, and other conditions. **Tapping lowers cortisol (the stress hormone) by 43 percent.**
- Tapping can be helpful in **multiple situations**. The first is when confronted with **the daily irritants of life**. The second is in the context of **limiting beliefs or repeated negative patterns.**
- **From reducing anxiety, regulating emotions, breaking away from cycles of obsessive thinking, to increasing awareness, improving perception of events, and speeding up physical healing**, journaling is a very well-known and extremely positive concept when it comes to an healthy mental state.
- Visualization can help **you gain confidence, enhance performance, boost motivation, decrease anxiety, and reduce stress.**
- Guided meditation **harnesses the power of your mind to attain your desired outcomes.**
- These tools will help you **uplevel** and **continue to grow.**
- **Your commute is an ideal time** to use one or a combination of these tools.

Chapter 6

Conclusion

You have in your hands a turnkey solution to access **MORE** of your life and get **MORE** out of life. Whether you elect to microdose psilocybin or not, **this program will reboot your life experience.**

If you decide to microdose psilocybin, it will help you by **lowering your ego barriers**, making The Microdose Diet even more efficient.

The combination of microdosing, tapping, journaling, visualization, and guided meditation is **unbelievably powerful, quick, and fun**. Since using this regimen myself, I have never experienced so much ease, freedom, and success in my life. I now let my unconscious mind do the work and it comes up with way better and faster solutions that I could have consciously. Then, I just have to execute, tapping into my increased performance abilities.

I believe this **ease, freedom, and success can be yours too.**

My aim with ***MORE!*** is to support you in making your **own informed decisions when it comes to reaching more of your potential**. I believe the information presented in this book will do just that.

> **"The important thing is to never stop questioning."**
> **–Albert Einstein**

As per Euripides, **"Question everything. Learn something. Answer nothing."** By harnessing your critical thinking ability, you will decondition your mind and body, creating space for more success, passion, and happiness.

Learn about The Microdose Diet products.

Section 2

Your 90 Day Microdose Diet

Chapter 1

Introduction

Throughout the next ninety days, you will complete exercises to calm your body and mind to help get off auto-pilot, release blocked emotions, uninstall automatic responses, and purposefully **install a new software aligned with your vision** and authentic self.

It is imperative that you calm your body as you rewire your brain. As mentioned in section 1 the body-mind connection is so strong that you can't rewire the brain without calming the body at the same time, and vice versa. When your body is in fight, flight, or freeze, meaning your nervous system is in a state of stress assuming that everything around is a threat, which is the case for most of us most of the time, you can't expect your mind to make any decision that's supportive of your success. Your auto-pilot mechanisms kick in automatically to save you from the real or perceived threats and you are now just reacting based on that autopilot mode. This reaction might save your life, such as jumping off the road at the sound of a speeding car. It might harm you as well, such as going in default mode of deep anger when mildly criticized by your boss. You will work to **remove these autopilot mechanisms from the default settings**, giving you access to them in case of emergency (such as life-threatening situations), and replace them with more beneficial autopilot mechanisms (feeling calm, safe, worthy).

This is why The Microdose Diet is so powerful. **You are working on your emotions, beliefs, and nervous system at the same time, from multiple angles.** You will still have memories of negative events, but their emotional charge will be greatly diminished, giving you the ability to act, not react. By getting off the autopilot, you will be able to make choices that are best for you.

Your automatic reactions were what was best for you when you were a young child. However, these programs were set up before you were seven years old, when your brain and nervous system were not capable of handling challenging situations. Hence, the flawed programs that are ruling all of us when the right buttons are pushed. I am criticized, I get into a fit of anger. I am at risk of being rejected, so I leave first. I am afraid to be humiliated, I make the first move and self-sabotage myself with an acidic comment.

It is an inside job.

I am sure that if you put this book aside and examine your life for a moment, you will see patterns of automatic reactions such as the ones mentioned above. Which, by the way, were some of my old patterns and behaviors. It is very challenging work to realize that **we hurt ourselves very badly with these pre-programmed responses**. For me, realizing that not only was I given plenty of opportunities that I overlooked, but that I also self-sabotaged them was heart-breaking. What was also heart-breaking was to realize why I had developed these subconscious programs. The perception of neglect, humiliation, rejection, hurt, and abandonment I had felt as a kid were the underlying reasons I had developed all these protection mechanisms.

When this realization occurs, we want apologies, acknowledgment, and contrition. However, this is very unlikely to happen. First, because the caregivers "responsible" for these feelings were doing the best they could (no matter how little that seemed to be to us today). More importantly, because it is **our perception of what happened** that triggered these programs. This perception may have been absolutely, or at least partially, flawed.

> **"Perception precedes reality." –Andy Warhol**

It is actually not necessary to open the Pandora's box of explanations with your caregivers to release these old patterns. What is necessary though is to have compassion for the young child you once were, the one who believed they had to protect themselves to survive (figuratively or literally). Validating your feelings that have likely been buried deep down is a key part of seeing success. Knowing at this point, even if just intellectually, that **you are worthy and that your feelings are real is very important**.

Too often, kids are invalidated. They fall or fail and parents dismiss it as if it was not important. But for the child, this is very important. And this is when children start thinking that what they feel or think is flawed and that, by extension, they are flawed. Hence, all of us walking with this big signage saying "I am not good enough," which not only **prevents us from being successful, but also prevents us from even trying**. This influences us to make choices that will constantly confirm this belief that we are not good enough. "I am not good enough of a parent," says the father who abdicates on his role. "I am not good enough of an employee," says the individual who opts out of the workplace. "I am not good enough of a player," says the child who stops tennis practices. And so on.

On one hand, this dynamic is extremely sad, but on the other hand, it is extremely powerful. Imagine using these fabulous unconscious mechanisms to your advantage, fully harnessing your subconscious mind to do your bidding. What if your subconscious mind was reprogrammed to "I am a fabulous executive, entrepreneur, student, parent, friend, player, and so on," or "I deserve tremendous success"? **How would your life be changed if the winds of your subconscious mind were now behind you, supporting you, versus in front of you, hindering you.**

Could that mean less work and better results? Would removing the foot that is constantly pressing the brake make you a faster and more efficient driver? Wouldn't the ride be more pleasant?

Removing the foot off the brake pedal is exactly what you are going to do in the next ninety days. And I assure you—no—I guarantee you that if you are following this diet as it is presented in the next pages, your life and, more importantly, the perception of your life will change.

A famous French hypnotist, Camille Griselin, used to say that **"In life we don't get what we deserve, we get what we believe we deserve."** So let's make sure your beliefs are congruent with your desires, and that your emotions and nervous system utterly support these new beliefs.

When it comes to the program itself, you'll notice that you won't begin ingesting psilocybin until Week 4. The reason for this is because it is first necessary to do a lot of clearing. You're probably familiar with Marie Kondo, the well-known organizing consultant and author of the hit book *The Life-Changing Magic of Tidying Up*. I could never understand why the concept of decluttering was so popular. That was until I realized that if I wanted new things in my life, I needed to make space for them. At this stage in my microdosing process, I know that it is actually **more important to clear the crap than to bring in new things**. After all, the new things will only feel exciting and fresh if the garbage has been taken out first.

If you follow the 90 Day Microdose Diet purposefully, **you will get closer to your vision**, regain your appetite for life, discover excitement for the days ahead, and experience more love for yourself and others. Ninety days is nothing. Make the effort. You Only Live Once!

Watch a video and learn about some of the benefits linked to the The Microdose Diet.

Chapter 2

Top 10 Reasons Transformation Doesn't Happen

If you are holding this book in your hands, it is extremely likely that this is not your first attempt at change or transformation in order to experience more success. You have been looking for more in your life, which makes us kindred spirits. It is also very likely that **you have failed, more or less miserably, in your previous attempts at creating change**. If this is the case, once again, we are kindred spirits. Considering that The Microdose Diet is a bit more innovative than the traditional "get up at 5 o'clock in the morning, meditate, say affirmations, and build a vision board." I assume that you are coming to this work with high expectations, but also skepticism due to your past failed attempts. That's fine!

High expectations and skepticism were my middle names too when I started this process. And here I am, putting everything on the line to share this protocol with you. This is how much I believe it is a game-changer for humanity.

However, I am also mindful of the blocks to effective transformation, no matter how excellent the program. Indeed, through both my own experience and work with others, I've **observed ten reasons personal transformation for success might not happen**. By being aware of them, you can be mindful about avoiding these common pitfalls.

1. YOU SEEK PERFECTION BEFORE TAKING THE LEAP

It is very common, especially for Type A people who are used to control and aim at perfection, to believe that **everything needs to first be perfectly understood, contained, and laid out correctly before engaging in any activity**. After all, this approach is what likely made you as successful as you are today. Unfortunately, in this context, and I am afraid to say in most contexts, this attitude smothers any type of creativity, serendipity, and overall opportunity. I know as well as the next person that, in most cases, controlling feels like the only way and that just thinking about "opening up to possibilities" can lead to heart palpitations. Real heart palpitations. Alongside blushing and sweating. What your mind can create is quite amazing when you really think of it! Again, let's make this brilliant mind work for you, versus against you.

I totally understand that your unconscious mind is already rebelling at the idea of not controlling everything from the beginning to the end of the process to get perfect results, even before having started. This is one of the challenges we will address in the program. Again, I realize this is scary, but control and perfection have brought you where you are. **If you want more of life this will have to change, ever so slightly.** Keep in mind that done is better than perfect, so let's get started with enthusiasm and abandon (or at least 5 percent less control!).

If you don't change what you're doing, nothing in your life will change.

2. YOU HAVE LIMITING BELIEFS REGARDING YOUR ABILITY TO CHANGE QUICKLY, SAFELY, AND EASILY

Believing that it is slow and challenging to change is also a foundational block developed during your childhood, a defense mechanism which aimed to keep you safe. The corollary to "let's control everything to be perfect" is "change is painful." Indeed, this little brain of yours really loves you very much and **has put in place a whole bunch of unconscious beliefs aimed at keeping you safely in your little box.** The challenge is when you want to get out of that small little box to explore the big brave exciting world out there to get more out of life you are faced with these unconscious beliefs which block your success. The merry-go-round of one step forward, one step back then starts. You will try something new and really give it your all: learn a new language, take a new leadership course, eat healthy, go to the gym, and then, at some point, unbeknownst to you, it unravels. And when comparing your end results to the efforts and resources you have allocated to this endeavor, this will be, at best, underwhelming. We all know that roughly 90 percent of people who lose a lot of weight eventually regain just about all of it.[39] We also know that 70 percent of lottery winners end up broke and a third go on to declare bankruptcy.[40]

This is the result of your subconscious in action telling you that it is not safe to change, to go outside your zone of comfort. That you are an overweight person or a $100K a year person, and this spot is where you are safe and secure. **Slimmer and wealthier are unfamiliar and unsafe for your subconscious.**

We will work to release this belief that change is unsafe throughout this program. **Without this work, you will be paddling upstream toward success, rather than finding ease and enjoyment in your life.** Now you start seeing why you have had such underwhelming results with all the programs you tried in the past! The Microdose Diet really is the foundation to any kind of personal or professional development. Don't waste time training, studying, working, and dieting without having dealt first with this flurry of emotional, mental, and physical blocks. Best case scenario, you will spend tremendous amounts of effort for very little results. Worst case scenario, you will spend tremendous amounts of effort for very little results, be depressed, and give up any hope of ever accomplishing your dreams.

Working hard for success without having released first your fear of change is a waste of resources.

3. YOU ARE NOT CONGRUENT IN YOUR ACTIONS, WORDS, THOUGHTS, AND GOALS

Think of your unconscious mind as a super spy. **It is always watching and listening to you.** Not because it is mean, but because it wants to be of service (and keep you safe! If you die, it dies and it doesn't want to die). We all have this friend (and it is so much easier to see this in others than in ourselves) who wants the big job but refuses to move to a big city, doesn't want to work after 5:00 p.m., and won't even apply for new roles. It is very easy for us to see that they are likely not very committed to their goal. In this case, their unconscious mind is both an actor and a viewer, reinforcing each other. The actor has the flurry of limiting beliefs and emotional wounds working in the background to prevent the individual from taking the right actions in alignment with their goal. And the viewer notices every time an action incongruent with the goal happens, in this case, not actively pursuing job opportunities.

If we apply this principle to The Microdose Diet, your unconscious mind might hear you telling relatives about this amazing new program that will change your life. But when not seeing you doing the exercises, **it will conclude that transformation is not that important to you and will move on to something else.**

The lack of congruence is a big trap as **it is at the same time a cause and a symptom of your unconscious mind's flawed programming.** So start observing yourself. Do you say things contrary to your goals by habit or to look socially acceptable? Do you take actions that will prevent you from reaching your dreams just because you are on auto-pilot?

Becoming congruent with your vision, even in very small ways, will go a long way to support your success.

4. YOU ARE MORE ATTACHED TO THE PROCESS THAN TO THE INTENTION

This can also be a complement to "wanting everything perfect and controlled." Your focus is on the steps to follow. **You believe the**

magic is in the process and forget why you are doing what you are doing. The "how" became more important than the "why." You are following a recipe blindly, not deviating by an iota, and never coming back to your intention of why you are even doing what you are doing. Again, this is very frequent in type A personalities who tend to be focused on getting the job done: "Give me a target, a method, and I will execute it flawlessly." This approach works well for tasks that are less about the spirit of the law than the letter of the law.

However, this is not the situation we are dealing with here. Just going through the motions won't cut it. We need the heart, the mind, and every fiber of your being engaged. **This is not a mindless task; this is your life.** To maximize your results, I want you to stay connected to your why. I also want you to be mindful that if there are some exercises that are hitting on a big rock (or rather, boulder for you) you can (and should) spend more time on it. You should be able to adapt (slightly) the process to suit your own situation when necessary.

Focus on your "Why" versus the "How."

5. YOU HAVE UNREALISTIC EXPECTATIONS

It has taken you decades to build the layers of conditioning, rules, and beliefs that make you who you are. You will not unlearn all of that overnight. This program will bring you to the next level in your life. It won't bring you to the ultimate level. You won't become a mix of the Dalai Lama, Oprah Winfrey, Tom Cruise, and Serena Williams in ninety days. **You will become a way better version of yourself in absolute and relative terms.** However, there will be work for you to do for the rest of your life to become your ultimate version. It is not a one time, done and done. You can follow

The Microdose Diet multiple times. Every time you do so, you will go deeper and the positive results will continue to unfold. I will also publish additional books focusing on specific challenges, including money, weight, health, and relationships. There will be plenty of topics you will be able to address eventually.

This is a marathon. And within this marathon called life, you can engage in multiple sprints with the help of The Microdose Diet. So your overall marathon, goes faster, longer, and better.

No overnight success is in sight.

6. YOU SEE THE MICRODOSE DIET AS A LINEAR PROCESS RATHER THAN A SPIRAL

In a healing and growth process, once you clear something away, **it might pop up again at a higher level of consciousness** (or what we can refer to as a less conditioned mind), especially if it was a very big rock. Think about it like this: you've studied math for probably fifteen years of your life. It was always characterized as "math" but each year you went a level deeper. This didn't mean you were allowed to forget everything you learned in the ninth year when you made it to the tenth, nor that you could skip from year two to year seven. It's a process of continuous growth.

Similarly with The Microdose Diet, you will clear some blocks that you might not have been conscious of having. As your life goes on or as you go through a second iteration of The Microdose Diet, the same topic is likely to pop up again. This will feel surprising, frustrating, and probably upsetting as you thought you were done with this. But like math, you are now at a more senior level when it comes to your own self-awareness (meaning less auto-pilot) and **this challenge will need to be cleared again**

at this level. Hence, the spiral versus the straight line. You should not worry, you are not doing anything wrong, the clearing is working, you just had more to clear that you could not access before.

This is the process. I used to be very frustrated by that, thinking that I was not doing things "properly." One day, as I was following the excellent Duality program from Jeffrey Allen on Mindvalley, one of the participants asked this very question: "Why is it that I keep clearing old emotions and blockages related to my ex-girlfriend?" He was from the opinion (like me, at the time) that once a clearing was done, it was done, and you could move on. This is when Jeffrey explained the spiral approach. Growth is not a straight line, but an upward spiral. Even if the overall trajectory is up, we move back and forth between dark and light, conflicts and resolutions, one step back to one step forward, similarly to the shape of a spiral. It was an eye-opening moment for me which relieved me from a lot of frustration. Indeed, I had to clear some events multiple times over the years, but **these events had such a significant impact on my beliefs, emotions, and nervous system that they shaped me at a very deep level.** Uprooting them requires going through layers and layers of wrong assumptions, automatic answers, shocks to the system, and so on. Now every time one of them pops up, I know that I have done a great job and that I am going deeper in removing the remaining roots.

Transformation is not a straight line.

7. YOU LACK GRATITUDE OR RECOGNITION OF CHANGES

I am not referring here to #gratitudeformybeautifullife on social media for having a cup of coffee in the morning. It's great if you are sincerely grateful for the beauty of life, but if you are like me, I doubt very much that you sincerely are. **Maybe glimpses of gratitude show up here and there**, but I have yet to meet individuals in constant or even frequent states of gratitude. And if they are, they are not posting their lives on Instagram. They are busy enjoying and experiencing them!

I am referring to **acknowledging your progress, no matter how small**. You are likely going to miss the changes that have been occurring in you and your environment if your expectations are unrealistic (as seen in the previous mentioned limiting belief number 5 "You have unrealistic expectations"). However, recognizing and being thankful (toward yourself) for the changes is very helpful for this process. First, it keeps you motivated to follow the program. Second, it is telling your mind, who is always watching, that it works and that you are successful. Third, it uplifts you.

This is why the journal prompts are so important (please do them!). **By reflecting on your progress, you make them more real.** Your subconscious is now looking for things that are working well, versus what is not. The more it looks, the more it finds. Focusing your attention on your progress will generate more progress. Just thinking about your headways is not enough, write about them. It doesn't have to be a book, but writing makes changes more tangible for both your conscious and unconscious mind.

I am of two minds when it comes to sharing with friends and family members the progress made. Unless you have some like-minded individuals in your inner circle, you will likely meet naysayers inclined to pee on your parade, which will be damaging to your growth. It can be a good test, though, to see who around you are people who want to uplift you and who are not so

Focus your mind on what is working and it will actively support your growth.

keen. Remember, **misery likes company and you are the company you keep.**

8. YOU DON'T BELIEVE YOUR PROBLEMS ARE BIG ENOUGH TO BE ADDRESSED

This belief is unfortunately widespread and dipped in guilt: "How could I complain about my life while so many people have such a difficult life?!" First, this is not about complaining, blaming, or shaming. It is about growth and fully living out your potential. Second, these two concepts are not mutually exclusive. It can be true at the same time that some people have a horrible life experience and, at the same time, that you want to achieve your personal potential. You not achieving your potential by being free from limitations won't make people's lives worse. In fact, I would argue the contrary. Justifying poor self-care and self-love by the fact that others have difficult lives is simply another misguided limiting belief. My religious education, which was long and let's be honest, akin to brainwashing, has put in my head a lot of similar beliefs that absolutely don't help anyone. Not me and not the underprivileged. **It did prevent me from asking questions, looking for answers, and growing for a long time though, keeping me obedient, with a fixed-mindset.** But this was absolutely not for my greater good.

Again, it's easy to think that others have it worse and you shouldn't be complaining. There are multiple truths that can co-exist simultaneously. Others might have had a harder time, but **you still deserve to release your limiting beliefs and emotional traumas**. The two things really have nothing to do with each other, even if it seems like it.

If you have picked up this book, it is because you believe that you can and should get more out of life. This is the right attitude! **Why on earth should you be ashamed for wanting to make the most of your life.** You will likely inspire others to do the same and make the world a better place thanks to your efforts toward success and self-actualization. Congratulate yourself for making the efforts that will benefit not only yourself but also your family, friends, colleagues, neighbors, and anyone who will come into contact with you.

You deserve growth and success. Absolutely and relatively.

Last but not least, even if you were the only one to benefit from this personal growth, this is still great. You deserve it and you are worthy of it. **You don't have to justify yourself for doing anything that will be good for you.** Period.

9. YOU LET SKEPTICS INTO YOUR HEAD

As I mentioned briefly in the previous limiting belief number 7 "You lack gratitude or recognition of changes", I am ambivalent when it comes to sharing hopes, plans, beliefs, and progress with others. On one hand, having deep discussions with like-minded individuals can generate growth, accelerate and support your transformation. On the other hand, and this is where I am going with this point, like-minded individuals are few and far between. You will likely end up opening up your kimono with **people who will turn out to be unsupportive for their own personal reasons that have nothing to do with you**. This is the biggest growth-killer. Friends and family members demeaning your efforts, invalidating your beliefs, and mocking your progress. Don't go there.

Over the years, I have been fortunate to meet a number of like-minded individuals with whom I can share my endeavors. But even then, I am very careful with what I am sharing and with whom. **Some friends are very good with some aspects of my growth, but get very passive-aggressive when it comes to other areas.** You know what? I don't need that. And you don't either.

When in doubt, just keep your efforts to yourself. **And in no time, others will see for themselves the changes and they will ask you what you did!**

Once you have achieved your vision, feel free to share the intention you had and the protocol you followed. Not before that, or at least do it very carefully.

10. YOU BELIEVE THAT ONE SIZE FITS ALL FOREVER

We have been trained to think that way with the **magic food diets**: "no meat for ninety days," "all meat for ninety days," "no gluten forever," "eat anything you want" and so on.

I have an allergic reaction to these statements. We all have different bodies, minds, health histories, backgrounds and so on; **how could one approach be optimal for everyone all the time?!** It just doesn't make any sense to me. What I was doing and taking three months ago is not even the best approach for me today.

I am a big supporter of Heraclitus' perspective: **"No man ever steps in the same river twice, for it's not the same river and he's not the same man."** Not even the same regimen would work in the same way for the same individual all the time. I understand that it feels like the easy button to have a simple and constant "way of doing things" that "guarantees" optimal results for everyone. But this is just untrue.

There is a reason I am using a combination of tools and methods in The Microdose Diet. **Optimal results require multi-pronged approaches that can be adapted to everyone's specific needs.** This is why I ask you to question everything, to spend more time on areas you believe you need more oomph. The Microdose Diet is about reclaiming your true personal power. This requires an independent mindset willing to question and adapt common knowledge for the best results.

If you are reading these lines, you are open-minded. **No one with a closed mind and a fixed mindset reads a professional development book that uses a combination of alternative medicines.** But you might forget that fact due to decades of hearing about this or that magical solution that performs miracles on everyone all the time without effort.

Ditch the one size fits all. **You are unique.** Trust your instincts. If you believe something works great for you or the contrary, follow your gut. No one knows yourself better than you, no matter what people try to tell you.

This is how people get conned by the Madoffs of this world. They tune out their instincts and follow the herd, looking for social acceptance. Big mistake. **This is also how medical errors happen, by giving our power away to the powers that be.**

Embrace your individuality and the fact that what might work for you might not work for your neighbor.

• • • • •

These ten reasons are there to guide you into more self-awareness as you embark on The Microdose Diet journey. Just these ten reasons give you very strong insights into your psyche, your mindset, and your emotions (or perceived lack thereof). I used to have a very fixed mindset. But in reality, I had a growth-oriented mindset that was shaped into a fixed-mindset by the adults around me. **I don't believe that any human being is born with a fixed mindset.** They are strongly influenced by the people, events, and circumstances of their childhood. They either keep their growth-mindset, or morph into a fixed-mindset to protect themselves from rejection, abandonment, humiliation, and so on.

If when reading these ten reasons you are thinking "this is absolutely me!" fret not! I was the picture-perfect of all of those, and I was able to free myself, starting by detecting that I had these beliefs. **You can't solve a challenge you don't know you have.** With The Microdose Diet, not only will you get a better view of your blocks, but you will also be able to release them at your current level of being. This is priceless and a life-long journey in becoming a more authentic version of yourself. You are embarking on a "Benjamin Button"-type trip, reclaiming who you authentically are (fucking amazing, let's be real here!), and letting go of who you had to become to be "acceptable" by your environment. Accepting who you are fully—the good, the bad, the excellent, and the ugly—is the key to becoming whole again. It is a challenging process to love and accept even our perceived flaws, especially when these perceived flaws are totally unconscious.

As an example, I was led to believe as a young kid that I was selfish for saving and investing money, that only boring people were investing their money and that I was wrong to act in that way. Of course, intellectually, I now know very well that these were highly flawed programs from an "interesting" caregiver, but how do you think my unconscious has been reacting over the years to any attempts at saving money? Yep, not well. All our programs are not as destructive and counter-intuitive as this one, but my point is that **you might unconsciously dislike a part of you that is not even socially unacceptable**. Like in my case, with despising my selfish, boring, shameful saver and investor aspects.

We have a lot of work to do together, as **you may be buried under decades of false beliefs, emotional wounds, stress, and anxiety that are keeping you stuck, and far—very far—from success, self-actualization, and achieving your potential**.

So let's get going and do some excavation work!

Listen to interviews of experts on The Microdose Diet podcast.

Key Takeaways - Chapter 2

Top 10 Reasons Transformation Doesn't Happen:

1. You **seek perfection** before taking the leap.
2. You have **limiting beliefs** regarding your ability to change quickly, safely, and easily.
3. You are **not congruent** in your actions, words, thoughts, and goals.
4. You are more **attached to the process** than to the intention.
5. You have **unrealistic expectations**.
6. You see The Microdose Diet as a **linear process** rather than a spiral.
7. You **lack gratitude** or recognition of changes.
8. You don't believe your problems are **big enough to be addressed**.
9. You let **skeptics** into your head.
10. You believe that **one size fits all forever**.

Top 10 Pieces of Advice on Transformation to Consider:

1. If you don't **change what you're doing**, nothing in your life will change.
2. Working hard for success without having **released first your fear of change** is a waste of resources.
3. **Becoming congruent** with your vision, even in very small ways, will go a long way to support your success.
4. **Focus on your "Why"** versus the "How."
5. **No overnight success** is in sight.
6. Transformation is **not a straight line**.
7. Focus your mind on **what is working** and it will actively support your growth.

8. You **deserve growth and success**. Absolutely and relatively.
9. Once you have achieved your vision, feel free to share the intention you had and the process you followed. **Not before** that, or at least very carefully.
10. **Embrace your individuality** and the fact that what might work for you, might not work for your neighbor.

Chapter 3

Week 1 – Assessment and Clearing

Welcome to Week 1!

I can't think of anything more awful than simply being the spectator of one's own life, rather than truly living it, of being incapable of viscerally experiencing your life as the main character of the most important story that has ever unfolded.

Paul Newman always had a sense of being an observer in his own life. **He had the sense that he was watching something, not living something.** I used to feel that way too—emotionally anesthetized. And I speak with so many high achievers who share this perception.

What could be sadder than this—observing one's life, but not experiencing it. **Living in total auto-pilot; a life built by conditioning, rules, and being socially acceptable.** What a shame!

When I look at all the years I have wasted not fully participating in my own life, reading and playing a script written by others for me, it really makes me angry. At the same time, it makes me happy and hopeful that I am not on the merry-go-round anymore and that **I regained my rightful place as the writer, actor, director, and producer of my life.**

If you too want to know how you could get off at the next stop, take back control of your life, write yourself the script of your own life, and finally experience your life firsthand, read on and please, pretty please, do the exercises! You will discover how **you can experience more success and get your real authentic life back**!

Before you begin, get a journal that you can dedicate just to this program.

Bear with me—I know what you're thinking. I too hate when I am told that I will need a journal (almost as much as when I am told I have to meditate). This is an important part of The 90 Day Microdose Diet, because microdosing provokes such subtle changes over time that you won't notice transformation overnight. Writing down your thoughts and feelings over the length of the process allows you to flip the pages back and think, "Wow—the language I used two weeks ago is so much more negative than it is today!" It's a bit like how some people take photos of their bodies after going to the gym each day. Because we live with ourselves twenty-four hours per day, seven days per week, it can be hard to see progress otherwise. In addition, journaling focuses your mind. Don't forget that your unconscious is always watching you. **By recording your progress, you are "brainwashing" yourself and your mind into getting more of what you want.**

INTENTION – YOUR WHY

On the first page of the journal, **write down your intention for The Microdose Diet**. You picked up this book because you wanted something specific. What is it? This is intended to be a vision, rather than a concrete goal. Make the intention as visible as possible and return to it during the days when there are parts of the diet you don't feel like doing. Again, we are making sure our unconscious picks up on our why frequently.

Intention and attention are two extremely important components of growth.

The intention is where you want your mind to focus long-term. Think about it as the overall strategy of "You inc.". This is your north star.

Attention is what you choose to notice. Where attention flows, energy follows. In "You inc.", attention will be tactical and short-term. You will put your attention to your progress, to where you want to go, to what you want more of.

During the next ninety days, I want you to **notice all of the positive events that are aligned with your vision and bringing you closer to it**. I am not saying that in ninety days you will jump from here to there, but the flow should start going in that direction.

ASSESSMENT – WHERE ARE YOU?

After you've identified your intention, it's time **to gain a better understanding of your starting point and begin the process of clearing out your body** to prepare for the benefits of The Microdose Diet to take hold.

I like to start with a simple assessment exercise. On the next page of your journal, write down ten different categories:

- Relationship with yourself
- Relationship with your partner
- Relationship with your family
- Relationship with others/the world around you
- Health
- Money
- Career
- Spirituality
- Leisure
- Zest for life

Rank yourself on a scale of 0-10 in each category. Don't overthink it. Write the first number that comes to your mind. No one has to see it. Do it for yourself. Then, calculate your overall score.

Is there an area that is dragging down your overall score, or are the scores fairly aligned between categories? **Can you identify any common threads between the various categories?**

When I did this exercise, I realized how often my own needs were put last, not met, or just unknown thanks to my people pleasing tendency. This was dragging my overall score by impacting multiple categories. My relationships with my partner, family, and others were not satisfactory as I thought I was not seen, heard, and validated. Similarly, in my career, I thought I didn't get the credit I deserved which was also impacting my money situation. My relationship with myself and zest for life were low as I was frustrated with myself, incapable of asking for what I wanted and feeling that I always had to be the good girl putting everyone and everything before myself. Then, it was easy to see that by addressing the underlying challenge—people-pleasing—**I could increase my satisfaction level in multiple categories and then overall.** For the people-pleaser out there, addressing people-pleasing is not easy nor is it a fast endeavor. However, being a foundational challenge, even a small improvement will greatly improve your life.

Do you have a foundational behavior that is permeating all of your categories? It is likely to be the case, so take the time for some introspection. Working on that aspect will bring improvement across the board. **This foundational behavior is rooted in limiting beliefs, emotional wounds, and is putting you in a defensive auto-pilot state.** When this comes up, you just react as the young child who installed that program.

Think about the patterns in your life. Have you been stuck in loops? Repeating the same actions, getting the same outcomes despite different people, events, and circumstances involved.

Are there parts of yourself or behaviors you exhibit that you deeply dislike? Are there qualities you were told you had as a kid (vivacious, bold, active, outspoken) that you really don't see in yourself anymore?

You want to understand the distance between this Authentic You and the Pretend You, this "you" you had to become to be accepted by your family, school, church, and society at large. Again, we are not here to blame or shame anyone. However, it is important to understand where you are coming from.

My Pretend Me was the people-pleaser, while my Authentic Me was the total opposite. Being born and raised in an intensely authoritative and twilight-zone like environment, my Authentic Me took it upon herself to transform into People Pleaser-Pretend Me in order to survive; I wanted to be accepted (or at least tolerated) in my microcosmos. This dichotomy created extreme self-hatred as well as mental health issues. **Becoming the polar opposite of who you naturally and authentically are is very detrimental to one's health and success.**

In fact, for the longest time, there has been a belief that mental health issues were something you were born with and that it was unchangeable. You were either mentally healthy or not. However, as per the Mayo Clinic, **certain factors such as traumas, a childhood history of abuse or neglect, and stressful situations are risk factors that can contribute to mental illness.**[41]

I meet many people every day who, during childhood, had to make tremendous changes to who their Authentic Self was in order to be accepted. Today, they don't understand why they have depression, anxiety, high-levels of stress, addictions, and other afflictions. **But how can one feel happy, optimistic, and be successful when they are living someone else's life because they were deemed so "wrong" or "bad" as a child that they had to make huge changes to who they were?** Very often, these people don't even realize that they transformed themselves to protect themselves. There are a few ways for you to recognize that you might be far from being your Authentic Self:

- Mental health issues, such as depression, anxiety, and addiction;
- High level of blame / criticism of self and others;
- Perfectionism for oneself or others;
- Deeply-rooted anger;
- Raging, judgmental, and negative self-talk;
- Self-sabotage;
- Very little memories of childhood.

As you are working on your assessment of where you are, don't just do the ranking exercise. Think about your childhood. Again, the point is not to blame your caregivers, but for you to **detect the blocks that are still at play in your life today, preventing you from fully using your potential and becoming as successful as you deserve.** Were you fully accepted as you were or were you frowned upon for being "different"?

I remember when I was a teenager, my friends were telling me that my mother was more of a friend than a mother. I could not really understand what that meant. Now looking back, I realize that indeed having a mother who tries to charm your parents' fathers, or your boyfriends, who lets a fifteen-year-old girl go out all night drinking and doesn't provide any parental advice is not really mother material. But at the time, I could not see this as I had been raised to be extremely obedient and submissive to my mother and anyone else by extension. The fact that my mother was narcissistic and that I had grown up in some odd parallel world where gaslighting was the rule only appeared to me when I was well into my forties.

You may not have had such a weird environment growing up, but you may have had a caregiver who was hell bent on you becoming an athlete, a doctor, heterosexual, married to someone from the same social class or race, and so on. These "preferences" were associated with not so subliminal messages that **if you wanted to keep the parental love and acceptance, you would be well inspired to follow the family model**. And that you would be labeled as bad or wrong should you choose to go in another direction.

Try to remember some of these trade-offs by recalling childhood memories. I have very little childhood memories which is usually a warning sign of trauma. However, I remembered being told by my aunt that I was very vivacious and ambitious, while my only memories were of being frightened, weak, and shy. One day (when I was in my thirties), I took it upon myself to ask my mother how I was as a child as I had no memories and they were quite contradictory. She lost her mind (surprise, surprise) and answered angrily that she had no other choice than "to break me as I was so spirited." Well, I guess here was a great hint to where the schism between the Authentic Me and the Pretend Me started! The reason for this story is not to blame my mother. She did what she could and in her mind she did well, or at least better than her own parents. The point is that **your perception of yourself as a child might be very flawed**. Having an honest third-party view would be helpful.

You can also think about the usual suspects when it comes to being told to become more socially acceptable; **look at the social class, race, gender, and religion that are not aligned with the powers that be in the place you grew up**.

All of this will help you detect the challenges that are permeating multiple categories and lowering your scores. **Being aware of these foundational issues will allow you to be more effective and successful with this program.**

I want to commend you for the work you decided to engage in with The Microdose Diet. **It will have a tremendous positive impact**, not just on you, but on anyone who is in your sphere of influence, such as children, spouses, friends, and colleagues.

CLEARING – MAKING SPACE FOR MORE GOOD IN YOUR LIFE

While the journaling exercises over the next twelve weeks will help you clear out your mind, we will **simultaneously put effort into clearing the body**.

During this first week, **gradually limit your intake of alcohol, tobacco, recreational drugs, sugar, and meat**. In parallel, increase your water intake, drink herbal cleansing teas, dry brush, go for a lymphatic massage (or regular massage), take an Epsom salt bath, eat fresh fruits and vegetables, work out and sweat, got to a sauna.

I know cleanses are very challenging, but we really want these **toxins to leave your body and brain as much as possible**.

Do your best to decrease the "bad" and increase the "good." I won't tell you to quit alcohol, sugar, and red meat cold turkey, but if you can that is amazing!

If you are really committed, which I hope you are, fast, do a juice cleanse, or a liver cleanse.

We want to make space for new, great, supporting thoughts, cells, and habits. If you are clogged up, it is impossible to add anything great. I know it is difficult, but you can do it! It is worth it! You are worth it!

We also want to give a message to your unconscious: **you are off the auto-pilot and you are committed to seeing your life change for the better**. As the weeks go on, I want you to continue to pay attention to this. Have the best healthy lifestyle you can have, while keeping your spirits up. I don't want you dejected. People who have an optimal healthy lifestyle but have sucked their zest for life in the process are missing the point of the cleanse. Do what works best for you.

When making healthy choices, remind yourself that you're doing it to create a better life. Try to make it a game. Compete with yourself. Have fun with it. It is always a question of framing. The most amazing activity framed as boring will be draining, while any mind-numbing activity performed with friends for a common goal will become fun, or at least not too bad!

Set yourself up for success: put the right music on, encourage yourself, smile, sing, do a little dance…you get it!

BONUS WORK – WATCH OUT FOR THE NEGATIVE EXAGGERATIONS

You know by now that your subconscious is always listening and watching you. This week, I want you to watch your words! **Avoid any negative exaggerations**, such as "the traffic is horrible; the food is disgusting; the show was awful." Every time you utter these words, you are anchoring yourself deeper in negativity.

You can even go one step further and **use positive exaggerations for the things you like**, or to compliment yourself or others. We can never have too much of those!

What are the ten energy vampires that suck you dry?

Key Takeaways - Chapter 3

- You picked up this book because you want something specific. What is it? This is **your intention, your vision, your why.**
- The **intention** is where you want your mind to focus on the **long-term**.
- **Attention** is what you choose to notice **every day**.
- You want your attention to be targeted to the events, no matter how small, that **supports your intention.**
- What are the **common threads in your life** that are preventing you from living your full potential? For me, it was constantly putting others first and myself second, a destructive pattern ingrained in me in childhood.
- Make space for new, great supporting thoughts, cells, and habits by clearing up your body and brain. **If you are clogged up, it is impossible to add anything great.**
- **Avoid any negative exaggerations.** Use positive exaggerations for the things you like.

Chapter 4

Week 2 – More Assessment and Clearing

Week 2 is all about getting deeper in your energy and joy assessment. We want to know what we are working with to be able to measure progress accurately.

ASSESSMENT – GOING DEEPER

When I started to be more intentional with my life, I put together a super quick map of **where I was allocating my time and energy** (see on page 106). It was an eye opener for me. I realized how much I was prioritizing people, activities, and places that were sucking the energy out of me, under the pretext of politeness, habits, and kindness. On the other hand, I was putting last what was making me feel joyful and energized. How selfish it would have been of me to actually do something good for myself!

The second exercise I want you to do as part of The 90 Day Microdose Diet is to create this exact same map for yourself to **understand your energy to joy payoff**. We all spend our time and energy doing things we both *have* to do (like work) and *want* to do (like spending time with friends). But it's not as simple as that: there is actually a whole spectrum of energy creating and energy sucking activities.

I recommend that you put together your own assessment over the course of a normal week or so to **evaluate** what people, activities**, and places are accretive (or not) to your lif**e. To do this exercise, write out the same ten categories you scored during the first week. Each day, pay attention to roughly how much time you devote to each category. Try to be as specific as you can. Rather than broad categories such as "work" or "time with relatives," opt for "answering emails," "meetings," or "playing board games with my nephew." Some activities can happen concurrently such as commuting and listening to an audiobook or calling your mother while walking.

Monday	Activity	Time	Level of Joy and Energy
Relationship with yourself	Listen to an audiobook	1 hour	High
	Journaling	15 min	Medium
Relationship with your partner	Date	1 hour	Medium
Relationship with your family	Call with Mom	30 min	Low
	Play soccer	30 min	High
Relationship with others/the world around you	Coffee Chat	30 min	High
Health	Stretch	10 min	High
Money	Pay invoices	15 min	Low
Career	Emails	1h30	Low
	Meetings	4 hours	Medium
	Write proposal	2 hours	High
	Commute	1h30	Low
Spirituality	Meditation	15 min	Medium
Leisure	Walk	1 hour	Medium
Zest for life	Watch funny videos	10 min	High

You can even go crazy and add additional layers of precision to assess **where your best returns and largest losses occur for the time and energy invested**. For example, grocery-shopping might only take two hours per week, but create a high energy loss. While cooking could be taking up to seven hours per week for a net sum game of zero in terms of joy and energetic value added. So the loss by unit of time related to grocery shopping is way higher than for cooking. If you really want to have a detailed picture, you can also take into consideration the energy input and not just the time input. Grocery shopping might be a low energy input while cooking is a high energy input, rebalancing the previous equation in terms of return on investment.

Monday	Activity	Time Invested	Energy Invested	Level of Joy and Energy Created	Return by unit of Time and Energy Invested
Relationship with yourself	Listen to an audiobook	1 hour *	Low	High	High
	Journaling	15 min	Medium	Medium	Medium
Relationship with your partner	Date	1 hour	High	Medium	Medium
Relationship with your family	Call with Mom	30 min **	High	Low	Low
	Play soccer	30 min	Low	High	High
Relationship with others/the world around you	Coffee Chat	30 min	Medium	High	High
Health	Stretch	10 min	Low	High	High
Money	Pay invoices	15 min	Low	Low	Low
Career	Emails	1h30	Low	Low	Low
	Meetings	4 hours	Medium	Medium	Medium
	Write proposal	2 hours	High	High	High
	Commute	1h30 *	Low	Low	Low
Spirituality	Meditation	15 min	Low	Medium	Medium
Leisure	Walk	1 hour **	Low	Medium	Medium
Zest for life	Watch funny videos	10 min	Low	High	High

* Activities happening concurrently
** Activities happening concurrently

This map is an easy way to grasp where too much time and energy are allocated to "losing" situations and where not enough time and energy are allocated to "winning" situations. Some of you might be (or at least believe to be) in situations with very little room to maneuver. Work would be a great example for most. I was myself an employee for many years and was feeling the pressure to conform and perform. But when I really took a step back, after doing this mapping exercise, I realized that I actually could not justify a lot of the activities I was supposed to do. I also realized that I had more power than I thought. I didn't really have to go to all the meetings I was invited to where my presence was objectively bringing no value, I didn't have to answer to all my emails in less than twenty-four hours to look like a top performer. The best proof was that many of my colleagues didn't and they were not less successful than I was by any stretch of imagination. Reversely, as an entrepreneur, the hustle culture is even more intense than the corporate life, in addition your income is totally dependent on your business. But here again you can choose to believe that you have to do whatever is strongly recommended by the current gurus or not. However, once you have done this map for yourself you realize that some activities that are supposedly the hallmark of successful entrepreneurs don't work for you (hello, 5am wake up call to work out, meditate, journal or intermittent fasting). Then it is time for you to be ruthless and just cut them. Obviously, the goal is to **redesign your life to minimize the energy-suck as much as possible, and maximize the energy boosts**. Keep in mind that your energy map will be very different from anyone else's, even if you have a lot of commonalities. What inspire you will not inspire others in the same way, and inversely.

In this example, listening to an audiobook while commuting has a high return on time and energy invested. Consequently, this is a practice that should be continued and prioritized. The date with your partner requires a high level of energy to only return a medium level of energy and joy. This begs the questions of "Was this a one-off," "Was the format of the date inappropriate?" "What can be made to improve the joy and energy created?" Emails require a low level of energy but also quite a bit of time to only bring a low level of joy and energy. Is there a way you could receive and answer fewer emails? Could there be a more efficient way to manage emails?

I would encourage you to **reflect on this map and adjust your activities accordingly**. Obviously, double down on the accretive activities. For the activities that are a zero sum game , is there a way for you to adjust them to make them more accretive or to simply cut them out and replace them by more value-adding activities? Activities such as cleaning are rarely uplifting. Could you afford some help? Even if you or your partner like "things to be done a certain way," I can guarantee you that having low value tasks done averagely by someone else is better than having it done perfectly by you. It might be worthwhile to cut out other expenses to afford the help too. Be creative! Are there people who systematically bring your energy level down? If you can't avoid them, try to see them less often, or around an activity that minimizes interactions (that's when spin classes come handy), or in a group. There are ways to manage toxic people who are unfortunately tied to you and your family. Now that you know what is working well, not so well, and not well at all, let the fun begin!

Your time is your time, and your energy is your energy. You don't owe them to anyone else. You can choose to allocate them a certain way, but you don't owe anyone anything. You obviously want to rise up to the level of your responsibilities, but I am sure that some adjustments, even small, can already boost the zest for life you are experiencing in your daily life. **You need time and energy for your own success. It is not selfish to take your needs and preferences into consideration.** You want to spend more time and energy on what brings you joy and reenergizes you. Inversely, you want to minimize what drains you.

One important thing is missing from this map: **the people, places, and activities that *would* bring you a lot of joy but have been cut from your life due to a lack of resources, limiting beliefs, or habits**. For example, I used to love curling up and getting lost for hours in a novel. By the time I became a working professional, however, I viewed fiction as an indulgence. This continued for decades; I engaged in reading fiction very rarely and with a lot of guilt (after all, I could be spending my time with something that was directly applicable to my career). This mindset failed to take into consideration that reading a good novel brings me a lot of joy. What are the things you loved doing as a kid? How could you intentionally incorporate them back into your life now?

Additionally, **trying out new things is a great way to find out if activities, people, and places not yet on your radar could be bringing you joy and energy**. You don't have to stick with them forever if you don't like them (or if there are things you like more). In 2023, I tried something new every month. In January it was cross-country skiing. I have always wanted to try it, but never made the effort to. I fell a lot and didn't really love it, but at least I tested it out. A new activity is also a great way to meet new people and discover new places. You can even rope in some family members and friends to make it a fun outing.

Ideally, pick activities that will bring you closer to your Authentic Self. For example, when I was a kid I loved playing sports, being outside, reading, writing, and animals, so in 2022, I added and increased activities such as playing tennis, volunteering at an animal shelter, reading, and writing. I also went out of my comfort zone by picking books I would not normally read, watching shows I never would have watched (reality TV, anyone?), and listening to podcasts that were out of my wheelhouse. The biggest change I made in the past years was obviously starting to microdose psychedelics.

We tend to have rigid ideas of who we are and what we like, but what if these ideas were not absolutely and utterly true? What if some activities that were "absolutely not you" would actually bring you tons of positive energy and joy? It is worth a try! Usually, it only requires a small change in our decision-making to forgo the usual default choice. I have always been more of a tomboy, so makeup has always been very minimal for me and I always thought that it was "so not me." In my attempts to switch things up, I started wearing lipstick, first nude and then red. I actually really like it, and it brings up a different aspect of myself that I have always dismissed. This didn't take a large amount of time or money and the risk was very minimal (compared with getting a tattoo!). It did allow me to bring more fun into my life though.

Some changes will require you to rock the boat, such as not spending the holidays with your family, for example (that is why vacations abroad exist!). However, if you feel miserable when doing so, what is the point in putting habits and conventions first? No one who loves you would want that for you. Keep in mind that when people push back it has nothing to do with you and everything to do with them. An example of this might be, "what would people think if we don't spend the holidays all together as a family?" Even if this time is dreaded by every relative.

All these changes, big and small, will bring you closer to realizing your potential and bringing you closer to your Authentic Self. That part of you that is still untouched by outside conditioning, limiting beliefs, and conventions. You want that part of you to grow bigger and ultimately be your entire Self. Being your Authentic Self is the only way to feel safe, secure, worthy, happy, and at peace, regardless of the external circumstances. This is your north star.

For me, making all these changes, writing a book, reading more, playing more sports, spending more time outside, but also spending less time on people, activities, and places that were at best a time suck and at worst toxic, gave me more energy, more joy, and more "lightness of being." **Being back in control of how I want to spent my time and energy versus blindly following my auto-pilot has ultimately given me a lot of freedom and personal power.** It can be the same for you!

The Passion Test by Jane Bray Atwood is a great book that I recommend if you want to spend more time exploring this topic.

Please note that **you can build the same type of map for your other resources**, such as money. Are you allocating too much money to activities or things that don't really bring high returns at the expense of more fulfilling activities? For example, too much money spent on shopping (low, short-term energy boosts), which crowds out the vacation budget (high, long-term energy boosts). This is a very valuable exercise. As mentioned, I will publish more books including one specifically targeted at money in the future.

CLEARING – OUT WITH THE OLD

Last week you started with clearing your body and hopefully you are continuing to do so this week! You can do it; make it fun! Create a competition with your friends. Who can reduce their sugar consumption the most this week? Including alcohol!

This week you are attacking your environment, or rather focusing your attention on your environment. **I want you to clear your space!** You have started to clear your body and mind; now is **the time to get rid of everything that is not aligned with your vision of success**. Old magazines, newspapers, books, clothes, knick-knacks—all of that needs to go. This will be fun! You are going to love it.

Decluttering is a great way to unstuck yourself. The goal is to create space for new opportunities.

Externally

This one is easy to understand. Get rid of the stuff you don't like, the stuff you don't use, and the stuff you didn't even know you owned. **Donate, recycle, tailor, mend, there are plenty of ways to make these items useful for yourself and others.**

I had this massive locker that was costing me $350.00 per month that I kept for years. It was filled with books, clothes, inventory from a failed business, and other stuff. I didn't even know what was in there and would have rather bought a new set of weights than trying to find them in the mountains of boxes. Every month I was complaining about the cost, about having to empty it and every month I was not doing anything about it. One day, I just gave my notice so I would not have any other choice than to empty it. It took me a few days, many trips to the Salvation Army and clothing bins, but I eventually did it. Some clothes were brand new and I am sure they made some people happy. **Now, I don't have to pay, nor think about it anymore.**

It takes physical and mental space to have clutter and unfinished projects. It is better to come to terms with the fact that some of these projects seemed cool (who doesn't want a home microbrewery, a gym, or spa-like equipment?). But some are unrealistic and you may need to come to terms with the fact that no, you will never fit back into your pre-pandemic outfits and they are not useful as a reminder of that situation. All the unread books and magazines, clothes that are too small, healthy food you will never eat and so on **are taking space and making you feel guilty, taking up precious resources you could allocate elsewhere.**

Very often when we try to get unstuck, we add things—a new course, a new book, a new membership. However, starting with removing the old is the best way to create space for new opportunities.

Internally

Getting rid of useless stuff will also **create more space in your** mind as you won't constantly see it and think about it. You can also create more mental space with more thoughtful to-do lists, email, and schedule management.

I used to have these two-page long to-do lists, with everything from the most important to the most menial and from the most urgent to the least. It was just making me feel constantly overwhelmed by the number of things I had to do. **Now my to-do list is very short and realistic.** If I don't really plan on doing something, or I will but in weeks or months, I just remove it. **I don't need aspirational items in my list sucking up my mental space and energy.**

Same thing with emails. I used to answer every email within twenty-four hours with very detailed and personalized answers. **Now I only answer what's important and urgent for me right away** and then I assess if the other messages warrant an answer or not. I have been saving so much headspace, guilt, and time!

I also lighten the load on my schedule *a lot*! **I learned to say no** (took me forty-plus years, but I did it!) **and put my own agenda first.**

My most productive time is in the morning. I keep that time for my creative work. Lunchtime is best for me for meetings, and afternoons for admin tasks. **I now organize my time accordingly, starting with my own rhythm and priorities in mind**, versus trying to accommodate everybody's schedules but mine.

Creativity needs space and getting unstuck is all about creating space and energy for new opportunities. Again, you don't have to add anything that will consume time, money, and energy. **Do less and do things differently; think less and think differently!** Quickly, you will see possibilities where previously you were only seeing blocks.

JOURNALING – REFLECT ON YOUR ASSESSMENTS AND CLEARING

You have done two different assessments of your life and engaged in two types of clearing. How do you feel? What did you uncover? Are you always putting your needs last? Are you prioritizing activities that in the grand scheme of things don't matter? Are you depriving yourself of fun people and activities because you can't find the resources (but still allocate these resources to mindless or socially acceptable activities?).

Use these exercises to reflect and make changes, even ones that are extremely small. If you feel that you can't seem to be able to make changes, even small ones, in some areas of your life, Bingo, you've hit upon a block! This is a nugget. Are you afraid of being the "Bad Child" if you don't do or say something or if, on the contrary, you do or say something? I have seen so many people (including me) acting out of guilt and then resenting the individuals and themselves for putting others first. **The goal is not to hurt people, but to understand when and where you are draining your own energy and joy for others.** In some cases, this is the right thing to do; often in life, we need to step up in particular life circumstances. But this should not be a constant or even a regular occurrence.

These assessments should show you your green, orange, and red lights. One of the challenges I see most often is an inability to say no. Here is a great strategy that will help you ease into learning how to set boundaries. **When you are afraid to say no to someone, ask for time to think about the request.** It will help you not react in your preprogrammed way. The microdosing will also help you with that, by making you more present. You will not jump on auto-pilot right away. This is how you break old patterns.

When it comes to the clearing, do you find yourself lighter and more energized with a cleaner body and environment? **Can you start seeing more options?** You have been creating space for new thoughts, things, habits, and patterns to develop. Let's make sure they are supporting you in your quest for MORE!

BONUS WORK: WATCH OUT FOR THE NEGATIVE FIGURES OF SPEECH

Avoid any strong negative figures of speech such as; "that meeting is a pain in the neck; this presentation is killing me." This is catnip for your subconscious that loves a vivid picture! By making a connection between a physical ailment and an actual situation, you are suggesting to your unconscious what needs to be done (your wish is my command!). Now no wonder why your neck (or other parts of your body) are not doing so well!

How rich people think.

Key Takeaways - Chapter 4

- Evaluate which people, activities, and places are **accretive (or not) to your life.**
- Where are your **best returns and largest losses** for the time and energy invested?
- Redesign your life to **minimize the energy-suck** as much as possible, **and maximize the energy boosts.**
- **You need time and energy for your own success.** It is not selfish to take your needs and preferences into consideration first.
- What are the people, places, and activities that *would* bring you a lot of joy but **have been cut out of your life** due to lack of resources, limiting beliefs, or habits?
- **Trying out new things** is a great way to find out if activities, people, or places not yet on your radar could be bringing you joy and energy.
- Ideally, pick activities that will bring you **closer to your Authentic Self.**
- We also tend to have **rigid ideas of who we are and what we like**, but what if these ideas were not absolutely and utterly true?
- Some changes will **require you to rock the boat**, but it is worth it.
- All these changes, big and small, will bring you **closer to realizing your potential** and to your Authentic Self.
- Being back in control of how you want to spend your time and energy versus blindly following your auto-pilot will give you a lot of **freedom and personal power**.
- **Clear your space!** Get rid of everything that is not aligned with your vision of success. Donate, recycle, tailor, mend,

there are plenty of ways to make under-utilized items useful for yourself and others.

- Unused things are **taking up precious resources** you could allocate elsewhere.
- **When we try to get unstuck, we add new stuff, but** removing the old is the best way to create space for new opportunities.
- **Create more mental space** with more thoughtful to-do lists, email, and schedule management.
- **Do less and do things differently; think less and think differently!**
- When you are afraid to say no to someone, **ask for time to think about the request**.
- **Avoid any strong negative figures of speech.**

Chapter 5

Week 3 – Clarifying Your Vision of Success

ASSESSMENT AND ADJUSTMENT – HOLISTIC CHANGES

This week's objective is to **clarify what it means for you to experience more success**, passion, and happiness in your life.

Now that you have reflected on the individual results of the previous two assessments, **evaluate them concurrently**; what did you learn? What is the top area that you feel is dragging you down? What is missing? Do you feel that small adjustments could already be implemented right now?

Let's say that lack of time for yourself is the main challenge at this point in your life. With so many responsibilities, obligations, and things to do at home, at work, and everywhere in between, you feel that you are just going through the motions and barely keeping your head above water. Of course, passion and happiness have taken a back seat a long time ago, and it is highly likely that **you are not living to your potential either**.

Start to think about what would have to change to **create more alignment with your intention and desired state**.

Now, for your third exercise, **create your *ideal* energy map**. What would it look like for you to be firing on all cylinders across each of the ten areas? How would you ideally be spending your time? With whom? What would be added to your weekly list and what might drop off completely?

Remember that you are the average of the five people you spend the most time with! You might think that it is unrealistic and that you are so busy that nothing can possibly change (especially if lack of time is your main challenge). However, you need to start **thinking about what you desire in order to get your lovely grey cells to find creative solutions** to your situation and bring you closer to your intention. In addition, when you introduce the psilocybin next week, your creativity will be fired up and you want these creative juices to have a target!

What about spending the holidays with your family every other year, sharing the kids' drives to practice with another family, working from home two or three days a week, or hiring a cleaning person? These changes are highly feasible, no matter what you might think. Implementing such reasonable changes can already free up several hours per week and a full week of vacation for you every other year. And this is just the first step!

One important part of this process is to **note the resistances that are coming up**. The fear of confronting your parents or in-laws to tell them that this year you will spend the holidays without them. Or the guilt for asking to share the load of the drives to and from the kids' games every week (or multiple times a week). Or the shame for needing help at home. **None of these thoughts and feelings that are coming up are real.** What I mean by that is that they feel real right now and should be acknowledged, but they can be released and put off the default setting. You don't need to feel fear, guilt, and shame to toe the line and be a "good person." All these automated protective mechanisms and limiting beliefs that have been installed during childhood can be uninstalled and replaced by more beneficial programs. Again, this conditioning was consciously or unconsciously programmed at a time when you had very little say over your world. Now, you still keep defaulting to it as they appear to be The Truth. **The only Truth is that you owe it to yourself to live your biggest, brightest potential**, which doesn't mean ditching everything and everyone, but does mean taking a step back, dispassionately, and assessing what works for you and what doesn't.

My family comes from a very traditional background and at the time I was born in the late seventies, it was traditional for grown-up children to visit their parents on Sundays, usually for lunch and a sizeable chunk of the afternoon. Oddly enough, my mother was not very keen at the idea of spending every Sundays at her in-laws. She did what was very rare at the time; she decided that she will come some Sundays at random, so as not to give anyone any expectations. She mentioned often during my childhood that she had **reluctance for bowing to obligations and had developed her strategy of not setting up any habits with anyone in order to keep her agency**. As much as I used to be a people-pleaser, I made her philosophy mine. When I moved to Canada, contrary to most immigrants, I didn't spend most of my vacation coming back to France to visit friends and relatives. This way, every time I came back it was a surprise and no one felt the obligation to bend backwards to see me either. This makes the time spent there so much more valuable and precious, because we chose to spend it together (or not).

Frequently questioning why you are doing or not doing something is the best way to make sure you are not falling into habits that are not supporting you and are likely not supporting the people around you either; we are rarely at our best when doing things from a place of obligation. Doing things less often will bring you renewed energy. Again, I can see you thinking and saying to yourself, "Peggy, I hear you, but it is easy for you and impossible for me." Question why you are thinking that. Is it because having the discussions with your father, your mother-in-law, your spouse, your boss, or your kids seems so daunting that you would rather keep the status quo despite feeling miserable (or at least definitely not feeling good?) How is this state of affairs working out for you? **You can't live a fulfilling life and achieve your potential when you're constantly adjusting your choices and desires to everyone else's.** I know that well. I have been there. And I am absolutely not saying that you should drop your responsibilities and move to Copa Cabana. My point is that most of the obligations and must-dos you believe are non-negotiable, actually totally are, and you would be surprised to see how easy some of these conversations go. You will only regret not having them years ago!

The extent to which we live our lives fully is the extent to which we are able to have difficult discussions.

Once I had built my aspirational energy map and understood the areas I wanted to influence, I assessed my progress every day by scoring myself on three questions:

- Did I create or capitalize on energizing opportunities?
- Did I experience freedom by letting go of worries?

- Did I find joy by engaging with people and situations that are accretive?

This only takes a few minutes. The goal is to **tap yourself on the shoulder for a job well done, giving more reference points to your unconscious and conscious mind for the new beliefs and habits you are developing.** When it comes to the missed opportunities, you can always do better tomorrow, as long as you know what made you decide not to capitalize on them. Is there a pattern there you should be mindful of?

Depending on what your intention is, you might **assess your progress** based on the time you created for yourself, the revenues you generated, your freedom and joy related to certain activities, or the addition of new energy-promoting areas to your map.

CLEARING – GOING STRONG AND WIDE

In parallel, you will continue the **clearing of your body, mind, and space** (this also includes your car and office).

I want you to add another layer of clearing: your words. This is an extremely important part of the process. If you have been doing the bonus work, you have already started to watch what you tell yourself and others regarding the negative exaggerations and figures of speech. Great job! You understand that every time you are saying something, good or bad, your unconscious doesn't discriminate, you are brainwashing yourself. Why would you want to brainwash yourself with bad stuff? I understand that complaining is a socially acceptable bonding experience, however it drains the energy of all the parties involved, starting with you.

I challenge you to **hear yourself talk and catch yourself** before participating in "bitch fests," may they be about the weather, the new reorganization, your sister, or the cost of living.

You can start by just staying silent when caught in one of these discussions, and trying to reorient the discussions to a topic that's more uplifting, or leave.

I had a coffee with a friend recently who was going on and on about her family. After what I felt was a decent amount of time to empathize, I just changed the topic in a more life-affirming conversation. Her physiognomy totally changed and she left me an hour later totally energized. I did create some space at the beginning of our chat to share her thoughts, but when I realized that she was spiraling and nothing good would come out of this trail of thoughts, I redirected the conversation to a topic I knew we were both passionate about. It ended up being an uplifting time together where neither of us were left drained—quite the contrary.

It is important to create a safe environment for relatives and friends to express their deep feelings. However, after a while, this is not creating value for anyone—quite the contrary. **Instead of processing their thoughts and emotions, they spiral and become totally inhabited by their thoughts and feelings.** I love supporting people; however, I am not an emotional garbage and need to protect my own energy. When I spend time with people, I want my energy to go up—or at least not go down. Otherwise, I need to reassess the place these energy-vampires should have on my energy and joy map (hint: none or very little). It is normal for all of us to have periods in our lives when we need more friendly support, but it should not become a habit. **Have no pity for the "bitch fests" happening around you and cut them short as soon as you can.** This is a very important part of your clear cut approach. **You need all your energy to fulfill your potential and dreams.**

JOURNALING – REFLECT ON YOUR ASSESSMENTS AND CLEARING

Copy over your intention from the first page of your journal. Now that you have assessed where you were and where you want to be, **is your intention still aligned with the vision of success you have crystalized?** Did you realize that actually something else would bring you more bang for your buck? If so, adjust your intention.

I realized that the best intention for me and anyone I ever came into contact with was to **increase our level of self-generated self-worth and self-love.** This is the deep knowing that you are worthy and lovable no matter your job title, marital status, jean size, or bank account. This is about the most elusive feeling, but also the most important anyone can have. And, as I will elaborate in more detail later in the book, **one cannot expect great external success while not having the strong belief that they are internally worthy of it.**

In life, you don't get what you deserve, you get what you believe you deserve.

If you are not convinced about what your intention should be or what desired state you should target, trust me and go for **"more self-generated self-worth."** This intention will encompass every aspect of your life and positively impact the ten categories.

If the intention you have selected from the get-go was reinforced via the assessment exercises, that is great! Stick with it!

I also want you to reflect on any Aha! moments the exercises created. It can take some time to process and integrate these findings. **No one wants to face the fact that they would rather buy peace than experience great success.** Life is full of compromises, however strong personal boundaries based on one's own values (not one's conditioned values) are the foundations to fully living one's potential. It is worth the challenges of having the difficult discussions. The next few weeks will help you with building the ability to support yourself on your movement.

Last but not least, what will be your metric of success? I wrote earlier about assessing your progress based on the time you created for yourself, the revenues you generated, your freedom and joy related to certain activities, or the addition of new energy-promoting areas to your map. **Select what metrics would make the most sense for you and every week measure where you stand.** It might seem challenging for some intentions. For example, if you decided to increase your level of self-generated self-worth, you will likely have to use proxies as metrics, such as the time you allocate to yourself for self-care and pleasurable activities, or the time and resources allocated to life-affirming activities that benefit only yourself. The trick in that context would be to be guilt-free when engaging in these activities. When you have high levels of intrinsic self-worth you don't feel guilt or shame for spending time and money on yourself. You feel good for investing time and money on yourself as you know deep-down you are worth it. This will likely be a tall order for most of you and this program will help you lift the guilt and shame when and while you put yourself first.

The evaluation of the metrics this week will be the baselines you will use throughout the 90 Day Microdose Diet.

BONUS WORK: WATCH OUT FOR THE CRITICISMS

We continue on our movement of **being aware of what we put in our mouths and heads** (and others').

This week, we go after criticisms. **This goes for criticism of yourself and others**, such as; "I am too fat; he is such a loser; she is an ass."

Others are just mirrors of ourselves and criticisms are the projections of the parts of us we disapprove of. Every time you criticize someone you are actually criticizing yourself—and your unconscious picks up on the fact that this quality is unacceptable for you to embody.

If you want to make great progress in living a successful life, listen to your internal dialogues when it comes to yourself and others. **Are you full of praises or full of criticisms?** What is it that catches your eye? What can't you stand in others? These are nuggets. Don't repress them by beating yourself up for thinking these thoughts. The more you repress them, the more they come back. Think about a ball immersed under water. With enough pressure, it bounces back to the surface with tremendous violence (and usually at the most inopportune time!).

I will ask you later in the book to tap on these feelings, beliefs, and emotions. You will do some tapping in the coming weeks, but you can already tap based on what you have learned in section 1 on tapping. This will give you a head start on the program!

I want to briefly discuss **the tall poppy syndrome** and how it affects our lives when it comes to fully living our authentic lives and achieving our potential.

The tall poppy syndrome, or rather the approach of "cutting down the tall poppy" originated in Australia and New Zealand. However, I believe it is universal; this refers to **the habit of criticizing successful people**. We have all witnessed and played a part in this phenomenon as the critic, the criticized, and most likely both. This phenomenon is extremely detrimental to humanity for the very simple reason that **rejection causes intense pain for the people being rejected**. Our unconscious mind, being a miracle of irrational rationality, would do anything in its power (including perceived self-sabotage) in order to avoid the pain of rejection.

Hence the aversion, unbeknownst to most of us, to be successful thanks to the widespread tall poppy syndrome. Changing our default setting from "I will be rejected if I am successful" to **"I will be accepted and loved if I am successful"** is one of the many resets necessary for you to live the success you desire and deserve. If you think that you are immune to this limiting belief, think again. My fabulous coach, Lise Janelle, once tested one hundred success coaches regarding their belief that they would be safe if they were successful. Ninety-nine individuals believed that being successful was not right for them. **This gives you a very good understanding of how permeated this line of thinking is among us.** And they were success coaches!

If you need more proof of why your subconscious is hard at work to make you avoid both success and rejection, having equated one with the other, read on. Neuroscience researchers out of the University of Michigan demonstrated that **the brain processes rejection like it does physical injury**. Rejection literally hurts.[42]

Is this belief serving you or blocking you?

Key Takeaways - Chapter 5

- **Clarify** what it means for you to experience more success, passion, and happiness in your life.
- What would you have to **change to create more alignment** with your intention and desired state?
- Create your **ideal energy map**.
- Start thinking about **what you desire** in order to get your lovely grey cells to find creative solutions.
- One important part of this process is to note **the resistances** that are coming up.
- The only Truth is that **you owe it to yourself to live your biggest, brightest potential**.
- You **can't live a fulfilling life and achieve your potential** when constantly adjusting your choices and desires to everyone else's.
- The extent to which we live our lives fully is the extent to which we are able to **have difficult discussions**.
- You will continue the clearing of your body, mind, and space and **add the clearing of your words**.
- Hear yourself talk and **catch yourself** before participating in "bitch fests."
- Have no pity for the **"complaining parties"** happening around you and **cut them short** as soon as you can.
- You need **all your energy** to fulfill your potential and dreams.
- The best intention is to **increase your level of self-generated self-worth and self-love**.
- One cannot expect great external success while not having the strong belief that they are **internally worthy of it**.
- No one wants to face the fact that they would **rather buy peace than experience great success**.

- **Stop criticisms** of yourself and others.
- Others are just mirrors of ourselves and **criticisms are the projections of the parts of us we disapprove of**.
- **The tall poppy syndrome** refers to the habit of **criticizing successful people**.
- Rejection causes intense pain for the people being rejected. Hence **the aversion**, unbeknownst to most of us, to **be successful** thanks to the widespread tall poppy syndrome.

Chapter 6

Week 4 – Introducing Psilocybin

If you were unfamiliar with psychedelics and psilocybin (magic mushrooms) you have probably spent quite a bit of time on section 1 and online to gather more intelligence on these substances and their effects. **By now you should have enough information to make an informed decision on whether you want to microdose psilocybin or not.** This is a personal choice. In some parts of the world, psilocybin is legal. In others, it is not. Based on your location, it will be your personal judgment call to decide on what to do. I am not encouraging anyone to do anything illegal!

If you decide to microdose psilocybin, you read in section 1 how to do this in a safe and strategic way. You will need to ensure that the quality of the products you are using are of the highest grade (depending on your geography, you can access premium products at themicrodosediet.com) and that you are following the protocol. Taking more doses more often will not accelerate the process, so don't go there! Stick to the quantity and frequency recommended in this book and you will see great results fairly quickly, especially when combined with the weekly exercises. **The Microdose Diet has been optimized for maximum success.** As mentioned previously, microdosing psychedelics is not recommended for women who are pregnant or breastfeeding, minors, and people with significant mental health challenges such as schizophrenia. I encourage you to speak with your family doctor to discuss your personal risks prior to engaging in microdosing psilocybin.

If you decide not to microdose psilocybin, you will still get great benefits from following the exercises. **You will witness changes and more opportunities knocking at your door.** You will also have more creative ideas and zest for life. If you wish to calm your nervous system without using psychedelics, I have used supplements in the past that have been helpful to me, such as 5-HTP and Gaba. I have a personal preference for 5-HTP that, similarly to psilocybin, impact your serotonin; since serotonin helps regulate mood and behavior, 5-HTP can have a positive effect on sleep, mood, and anxiety. Again, ask your family doctor if these supplements are adapted to your personal situation.

Microdosing does NOT mean taking one small dose at random.

When microdosing psilocybin, the frequency, dosage, and your intention are your keys to success. This principle is true for any type of microdosing, not just microdosing psilocybin. Similarly, you wouldn't mindlessly take one tablet of Vitamin C and expect to see an instantaneous boost of energy lasting three months, right? Nor should you with microdosing.

To maximize your results, both short-term and long-term, it's not *just* about microdosing psilocybin; **it's about your commitment to move in an intentional way.**

Again, **this is a success book**. It is about you **mobilizing more of your potential**—mental, physical, emotional—so you can achieve your goals in the best possible ways.

When I read that to be successful I need to wake up at 5:00 a.m. and hustle, I am just not inspired. My first thought is, "This person lacks imagination" and then "Give me my money back."

Yes, there is no free lunch. For example, if I can now afford the fabulous beach house in the Hamptons I have been dreaming of my entire life, there will be some headaches—dealing with the real estate agent, the paperwork, working with the designer, and so on. The same thing applies if I get the big job I have been aiming for. I will have to travel more, do more public speaking, deal with more third parties, and likely have more difficult conversations. So yes, in that context, I agree with the hustle-minded proponents out there that **there will be some trade-offs to achieving success.**

Indeed, these are first-world problems, but for our conscious and subconscious minds, they are still problems. Our minds don't like problems. They make the mind feel unsafe.

When you decide that you will spend The Holidays in The Bahamas instead of in your hometown, crammed in your childhood bedroom for four days, this seems like a definite win. However, you will need to have had the challenging conversation with Mom or Dad to tell them that now this is how it will be. **So there is definitely a price to pay for making any change.**

This also applies to winning the lottery. Now you will have to deal with managing the money, everyone asking you for something, the jealousy, the resentment, and so on. **Any long-lasting change will require growth to manage it.**

However, the hustle culture of sleeping less and working more to have more success is not about growth. **It is just about more of the same input (working hours) in the hope of more of the same output (money).** It's not about getting a different output for a different type of input. It is a very dissimilar philosophy of success than the one presented in this book.

The Microdose Diet is about helping you to get out of your own way and start getting more out of your life, faster and easier. You will need to change and grow to do so. There is no magic wand. But **by removing your roadblocks, this is a scalable solution that has positive long-term impact in every area of your life.**

The Hustle Culture is based on a one size fits all, zero-sum game, and the law of diminishing returns. There is absolutely nothing of value there. If a growth hack is to sleep less and work more, I have yet to see the value of such advice. It is like going on a diet and being told to eat less, eat healthier, exercise more, and you will lose weight. It's so obvious that it becomes unhelpful. **Did I really need to pay an expert to articulate that for me?** What I want to know is how to let go of my addiction to sugar. You don't need the help from someone with a PhD in nutrition to understand that too much sugar is bad. But you need help to understand why you can't drop the sugar (and the weight) and more importantly how to do so. If there are tricks and shortcuts, such as not eating raw fruits and vegetables after 4:00 p.m., having dinner before 6:00 p.m., or not drinking water during your meals, these are what you want to learn from an expert. Not the obvious—eat less or work harder.

So here comes The Microdose Diet! With this program, I will give you specific tools that you can curate to your own life. This protocol is backed by science and I will help you understand the methods you can use that will take you to the next level in your life. These can be modified for each individual.

During this week, **we want to become more aware of the limiting beliefs that have blocked us.** Psilocybin is a wonderful tool to increase awareness, calm our nervous system, and create a perceived time buffer to act versus react.

MICRODOSING PSILOCYBIN – READY TO TAKE OFF

You've spent the past three weeks clearing out your mental and physical cobwebs to make room for psilocybin, and now you're ready to start incorporating it! This will probably feel like the scariest but most exciting moment of the diet, especially if you've never microdosed before. Again if you want to learn more about psychedelics before taking your decision, read section 2 "Your Psychedelic Education" and don't hesitate to complement this information with your own investigation. Then, **trust that you have done the research and put in the work to set yourself up for success.**

You will **ideally start your regimen on a day you don't have to work or do anything important**. It's highly unlikely that anything will come up, as the dose is at a sub-perception level, but it's helpful to have the peace of mind of knowing that you don't have to have a highly productive day while also trying something (potentially) brand new.

Start your regimen by taking 100mg of psilocybin in the morning on an empty stomach. I recommend that people use either a cap or an edible, just to make measurements as easy as possible. Some participants just drop it into their daily smoothie. For the next three weeks, we will take a dose only every three days. As an example, you would take 100mg on Saturday morning, then on Tuesday morning, then on Friday morning. You should not feel a high due to the tiny amount you are taking, but it's best to avoid any activities requiring driving or operating heavy machinery until you're certain you know how it will affect you.

As you ingest your psilocybin, open your journal and connect with your intention. Feel your excitement about embarking on this transformation. Again, we are using the power of your subconscious to maximize the results (and minimize the efforts).

If you feel concerned about microdosing in the mornings, then just do it at night! It will not be on an empty stomach, but better to have it done than to have it done perfectly.

A few months back, I ordered a product that was combining psilocybin with a large dose of adaptogens (Lion's Mane to be exact). However, even if the dosage of psilocybin was only 100mg, the usual dose I have been taking, the association of the different active ingredients made it feel way more potent. Instead of just discarding the bottle (or feeling "high" when taking it) I just started to take it at night. The interesting fact is that I started sleeping a bit more deeply (until our kitten decided to ring the alarm at 5:00 a.m. every morning) and having more vivid dreams. **So taking the microdose at night is a totally viable option if it feels more comfortable to you.**

What is presented in this book are solid guidelines. However, I want you to take your power back. You know your body better than anyone else. I don't want you to strongly deviate in terms of dosage and frequency, but if you want to experiment with different times of the day, the content of your stomach and so on, feel free to do so. The Microdose Diet is not a new religion that you need to follow to the letter of the law. On the contrary, we are interested here in the spirit of the law and in **you feeling more self-confidence vis-à-vis your personal choices**. I am not a Guru. If anyone is telling you that their way is the only way, that is a red flag. Science, thinking, philosophies, and everything evolve. Your body changes, all of that contributes to the need for more personalization of the standard guidelines. And only you can decide what you are comfortable or not comfortable with. You are always in control. Use more of your personal power when making decisions. **Not making a decision is making the decision that others know better what is best for you.** This is simply not true. This is again based on childhood conditioning. No one but you knows what is best for you. So yes, it is important to stay informed, and to understand best practices. However, **it is even more important to think for yourself**. If you remember only one thing from this book, may it be that!

GOING DEEPER – WHO IS THIS IDEAL YOU

This week isn't *just* about microdosing psilocybin! You'll also continue your work **identifying your blockers and clearing space for alignment with your desired state.** To help with that clearing, this week's exercise will require you to focus on the *things* that are out of alignment with your desired state.

We mostly know what to do, we just don't do it because of an internal tug of war between our conscious and our unconscious minds. In the long run, the unconscious mind wins every time. That is why after doing so well with food, money, and relationships, sometimes for years, we just fall off the wagon and go back to where we were. Because where we were or are is where our subconscious mind feels safe. And as crazy as it seems, our subconscious mind will sabotage us to protect us.

This is why it is so important to detect and release limiting beliefs. You will not will your way or "positively affirm" your way to success. First, **you need to remove the twenty-pound ankle weight you have been running with all your life**. When these ankle weights drop to five pounds, now we can add willpower and positive thinking. Before that, we are just reinforcing the determination of our subconscious mind and actually preparing ourselves for a nasty backlash.

If you say your intention out loud, how do you feel? Does it feel possible? Do you have a little voice in your head telling you that you will never be able to do it? That life is tough? That this is what it is? That it's too late? That it would be too much work? That you don't have the time? That people like you, whatever that means for you, don't get to be successful, joyful, and free? Again, what are the patterns in your life?

For me, it was boom and bust. I could not handle success. I could not handle calm and serenity either. Nor could I handle having large sums of money. It didn't take a genius to realize that my extremely chaotic and underprivileged childhood was the source of these patterns. It was familiar for my subconscious mind to be broke, unsuccessful, and worried. And **for our subconscious mind, familiar means safe**. As paradoxical as it might be to associate struggles with safety and comfort, it is what subconscious minds do! They confuse pain with pleasure, and safety with familiarity, based on childhood experiences. If you are like most people I have ever met, your caregivers did their absolute best, which was in 100 percent of the cases insufficient. This is not mutually exclusive for one to give their best and still fall dramatically short. No blame game here. They were humans and they were likely highly unaware and using their own childhood as a baseline for their caregiving expertise. Take someone with a childhood at a 2.5/10 in terms of best practices. Raising their own children at a 3.5/10, they actually feel pretty good about themselves! They beat their own childhood by a full point. However a 3.5/10 is hardly a great success. This is where most of us stand, **with a childhood that was very far from best practices**! Did anyone at home, at school, or at church deliberately try to make you feel, on a consistent basis, safe, abundant, powerful, hopeful, and successful? I am pretty sure your answer is a resounding "No!" This makes sense; they themselves don't even know how to feel safe, abundant, powerful, hopeful, and successful. Did they actively build your intrinsic self-love, self-worth, self-esteem, and self-confidence? Again, this is likely a big "No!" that you are shouting internally. **What you are doing with The Microdose Diet is looking at the reality right in the face.** The first step to change is to understand what needs to change. I have zero doubt in my mind that you need more self-generated self-worth, self-love, self-confidence, sense of intrinsic power, safety, abundance, optimism, and success. We want you to ooze all of that. **No one will offer you an opportunity to be successful if you feel like a failure.**

It is very important to focus on the self-generated self-worth versus external signs of validation. It is easy to feel like a success when you already are one. But what happens when you hit a bump in the road? Or when you want to move to the next level of success? You don't have the internal self-generated self-worth to stay the course as you rely on others' vision of yourself to assess your worth. That is not the game we are playing here.

Once you have looked at the reality in the face, let's change it and **create the self-generated sense of success which is the basis of any type of success**—academic, professional, personal, or spiritual.

The protocol of TMD will support you in all of that. Right now, we are zeroing in on the big gaps, specific to you.

It took me a very long time to recognize this boom and bust pattern for myself. I could always find external reasons to justify why the constant worries, financial troubles, and career highs and lows had nothing to do with me (and my subconscious). However, to get out of these exhausting cycles and start building something for myself, **I had to look at the reality right in the eye and realize that the only constant in this equation was me. And this is where the root of the challenge was.**

> **"The definition of insanity is doing the same thing over and over again and expecting a different result."**
> **–Albert Einstein**

You have allocated resources to The Microdose Diet because you want changes in your life. You want *more*. So now that you are committed, let's do it fully. Going halfway is also linked to limiting beliefs, such as fear of success, fear of failure, and feeling unsafe to shine. Realizing that you already have enough—enough education, training, experience, and skills—to be more successful than you are today is the first step. **There is no point in going after another ability to create more success. Let's start by maximizing the abilities you already possess.** Then, if you want to add more competencies, that is awesome; you will be ideally positioned to acquire and fully leverage them.

Now, think about the hypothetical person who possesses the ideal energy map you created last week. Would that person wear a particular thing? Eat a certain way? Keep their environment fresh and minimal?

Create the space physically and figuratively for new, better, and more aligned things to come. Start becoming the physical and mental embodiment of your success, your vision. Your subconscious sees you dressing sharper, being more energized, oozing more positivity, and it is taking notes: "It seems like we are on a different program now. Okay, I will look for ways for more of that to happen."

JOURNALING – WHAT ARE THE BARRIERS TO THE IDEAL YOU

This week, I want you to question everything and channel your inner detective. Awareness, awareness, awareness! Over the course of the ninety-day plan, new limiting beliefs will come into your awareness. I want you to write them down. You will clear them on a continuous basis. Think of them as multiple roots feeding giant weeds. We want to cut them down to get rid of the weeds. Some weeds will have more roots or stronger roots, so they will require repetition. That is fine and normal. You grew these weeds for decades. Some of them feel, for your subconscious, as real and as true as your name. So stick with the process!

Think about what has prevented you from already achieving success in the desired area of your life; Can you find people who, despite these barriers, have nonetheless been successful? Why is it different for you? Is it true? Does it have to be? Also jot down how you are feeling with the microdosing regimen. What are your success metrics?

BONUS WORK: WATCH OUT FOR THE DOUBLE NEGATIVES AND PREVENTION-BASED WORDS.

Say what you want versus what you don't want and use positive turns of phrase (versus double negatives).

For example, replace sentences such as "Don't be mean to your brother" with "Be kind to your brother" or "Don't fuck it up!" with "Give it 110 percent."

Keep a close eye, too, on your frame of mind when approaching a specific topic, as your language might translate your mindset by using disempowering, preventive words.

We are all experts at using language that is defeating and prevention-based, rather than empowering or promotion-based. Most of the time, we don't even realize it. **This prevention versus promotion language bias has a huge impact.** Excellent research published in the Harvard Business Review in 2017 showcased exactly how large this impact is in the venture capital world—the world I come from.

In this study, venture capitalists posed different types of questions to male and female entrepreneurs: they tended to ask men questions about the potential for gains and women about the potential for losses. Investors adopted what's called a *promotion* orientation when quizzing male entrepreneurs, which means they focused on hopes, achievements, advancement, and ideals. Conversely, when questioning female entrepreneurs, they embraced a *prevention* orientation, which is concerned with safety, responsibility, security, and vigilance. **This difference in questioning appears to have substantial funding consequences for startups.** Examining comparable companies, researchers observed that entrepreneurs who fielded mostly prevention questions went to raise an average of $2.3 million in aggregate funds for their startups through 2017—**about seven times less than the**

$16.8 million raised on average by entrepreneurs who were asked mostly promotion questions. In fact, for every additional prevention question asked of an entrepreneur, the startup raised a staggering *$3.8 million less*, on average.[43]

The point I want to make here is related to the importance of your language. Based on this research, you can assess exactly how much a prevention-based language is costing an entrepreneur. Now, let's extrapolate this to your life. **How much has your language cost you over the last year, the last ten years, or your entire life, in terms of missed revenue, sales, promotions, opportunities, raises—a staggering amount for sure.** So let's start today with a new promotion-based language! And if, like these female entrepreneurs, you are asked prevention-oriented questions, channel your inner politician and answer with promotion-oriented answers.

Why entrepreneurs and executives microdose psilocybin.

Key Takeaways - Chapter 6

- By now you should have enough information to make an informed decision on **whether you want to microdose psilocybin or not.**
- The Microdose Diet has been optimized for **maximum success.**
- You will witness **changes and more opportunities knocking at your door.**
- Microdosing does **NOT** mean taking one small dose at random.
- When microdosing psilocybin, **frequency, dosage, and intention are keys to success.**
- To maximize your results, both short-term and long-term, it's not *just* about microdosing psilocybin; it's about **your commitment to moving in an intentional way.**
- You want to **mobilize more of your potential**—mental, physical, and emotional—so you can achieve your goals in the best possible ways.
- Any long-lasting change will require **growth to manage it.**
- Start your regimen with **100mg of psilocybin** in the morning on an empty stomach, ideally on a day you don't have to work or do anything important.
- As you ingest your psilocybin, open your journal and **connect with your intention.**
- Not making a decision **is making the decision that others know better what is best for you.**
- We mostly know what to do, we just don't do it because of an **internal tug of war between our conscious and our unconscious minds.**

- To be successful and fulfill your potential, you need to **remove the twenty-pound ankle weight** you have been running with all your life.
- For our subconscious minds, familiar means safe.
- What you are doing with TMD is **looking at the reality right in the face**.
- **No one will offer you an opportunity to be successful if you feel like a failure.**
- It is very important to focus on **creating self-generated self-worth**, versus external signs of validation.
- I had to look at the reality right in the eye and realize that **the only constant in this equation was me**. And this is where the root of the challenge was.
- The definition of insanity **is doing the same thing over and over again and expecting a different result**. –Albert Einstein
- There is no point in going after another ability to create more success. Let's start by **maximizing the skills you already possess**.
- Think about what has prevented you from achieving success in the desired areas of your life; **can you find people who, despite these barriers, have nonetheless been successful**?
- **Say what you want** versus what you don't want and use positive turns of phrase.
- **Prevention versus promotion language bias** has a huge impact on your results.
- Entrepreneurs who fielded mostly prevention questions went on to **raise about seven times less** than the entrepreneurs who were asked mostly promotion questions.

- **How much has your language cost you over the last year, the last ten years, or your entire life** in terms of missed revenues, sales, promotions, opportunities, raises—a staggering amount for sure.

Chapter 7

Weeks 5–6 – Tapping Your Way to the Top

Week 5 is all about **calming down and feeling safe in being who you want to be**, doing what you want to do.

Your nervous system has likely been overtaxed for decades, starting in childhood. Hence, your current high level of stress, anxiety, and depression. Yes, this is all connected! Remember no man is an island. Similarly, everything in your body-mind is linked. You will experience mental and physical unease when your nervous system is constantly pressured. And this is a vicious cycle. **If your nervous system has been stuck in fight-flight-freeze in childhood, it will stay there, because this is its default setting.** This prevents you from getting out of the merry-go-round of high stress, anxiety, and depression, which in turn increases the demand on your nervous system. In order for you to get out and move on to a new baseline, we need to interrupt the loop.

We have two main goals this week. **The first is to calm you in absolute terms, when you are not engaged in any specific activity.** Think about it as level zero. It is highly likely that your level 0 is already akin to running in the Savannah trying to escape a lion, and more like an absolute 10. We want your level zero to become a "real" level zero in absolute terms, not in relative terms compared to an already extremely elevated baseline. You know that feeling when you arrive on vacation and you can't seem to be able to relax and it takes you half your vacation just to get in the groove? That is your level zero acting as a level ten. Even if you decrease it to a level five, it will already be a massive win for you. Remember, "Done is better than perfect."

The second goal is to make you feel safe and calm when you are going after your dreams and fulfilling your potential. This is definitely more advanced. Since we were born, you and I have been trained to believe that all sorts of things were wrong with us: being excited, being sad, being loud, being competitive, or to summarize it in two words, being alive. So what did your magical brain do? Wong associations! Again! If your environment wanted you to "be quiet and put everyone else's needs first," **your brain associated shining, being excited, and competition with rejection**. Because as a child, when you expressed these behaviors, you were faced with the entire gamut of disapproval from your caregivers, going from disappointment to resentment to anger to plain rejection. And that is not safe. That is very dangerous for a kid to displease their family members. In order to protect yourself, your little toddler–child brain that didn't know better put in place very effective mechanisms to make sure you would not engage in these dangerous behaviors. One of your immature subconscious' best tricks was to make you feel lousy in your body and mind so you would not be tempted to repeat these risky actions, so you would feel shame, guilt, stress, anxiety, belly aches, and the like when you would "act out." Now you wonder: "How is it that I self-sabotage myself by not even engaging in activities that would be beneficial to me or that I don't give 100 percent to?" Well here you are. **Your subconscious is playing "against you" by trying to protect you.** It is still on the default setting of your five year old self who would get the disapproving glance of the adults around her when being highly spirited.

This generates massive problems. First, **you are living the shadow of your life by only half-playing in a mini sandbox,** instead of going all in at Mudhdhoo Beach in The Maldives. Second, **you are creating significant mental anguish**. The internal tug of war happening within yourself is depleting you from your energy, enthusiasm, and zest for life. In their place, anger, resentment, hatred, and depression settled in.

You've been hacked!

If it was not clear to you before, it should be crystal clear now. You need to clear up the viruses of your old programs that are slowing you down. Not because Mommy and Daddy were bad people—they are also running their own software full of bugs—but because you are not really living your own life. **You are in a tiny simulation, playing a weak avatar created mindlessly by others.**

MICRODOSING – CONTINUE THE SAME PROTOCOL

For these next two weeks, we will stick with the same microdosing regimen as in Week 4: 100mg of psilocybin every three mornings. We continue to **calm your nervous system that has totally**

wreaked havoc for decades. Each time you take a dose, go back to your intention. Connect to your "why" and really feel it.

TAPPING – FEELING SAFE

One of the strategies I use for **clearing up the bugs and changing the default mode is tapping.** This is a tool that changed my life, and combined with microdosing psilocybin, it is nothing short of miraculous. If you are not familiar with tapping, fret not, you can learn more about it in section 1. You can also find a great trove on information on YouTube.

I was the living example of the "be quiet and put everyone else's needs first" conditioning, while my Authentic Self and Potential Self were saying "be bold and go for it 100 percent"; basically, a complete turnaround where **I had to become the exact opposite of who I was as soon as I could crawl.** The internal tension, self-hatred, depression, self-sabotage, and repressed anger it created in me was humongous. I have to give credit to my self-preservation instincts that I didn't implode or explode. On the bright side, it led me to understanding what had happened to me, and to writing this book, which I sincerely believe will help people.

Because I had to become such a different person, my many defense mechanisms were sounding an alarm every second of the day, just by having the audacity of taking a breath and probably making noise doing so (and "stealing" the air of someone else). I used to have so many deeply ingrained safety alerts that my subconscious was constantly screaming that it was not safe to do, say, or think pretty much anything. **No wonder I had such high levels of anxiety, stress, and depression!**

Both tapping and microdosing will help you to **calm your nervous system and remove the default settings of these protection mechanisms.** Your subconscious will still have the opportunity to access its old tricks when needed (next time you are running in the Savannah next to a lion, for example), but they won't be your default mode anymore. This gives you much more room to express and embody your Successful Self.

I want you to get off the "flight, fight, or freeze merry-go-round" you have been on for decades. Your tapping practice will also help you with **uncovering and releasing the limiting beliefs that are keeping you stuck.**

Please do the week 5 tapping exercise each day this week. If you can do it several times every day, even better. **As you tap, think about the situation you are trying to improve.** Memories or thoughts might come up as you tap; write them down and tap on them later. You can find the tapping scripts below as well as the online journey at TheMicrodoseDiet.com.

Please note that you **will likely experience physical reactions (yawning, hiccups, burping, coughing) when tapping.** This is excellent. The stuck emotions and energies are being cleared. This is what you want.

Of course, **these tapping scripts are general and aimed at helping the majority of the readers.** They will help you very much and you can also find great videos on YouTube if you want to add some variety and precision to your tapping.,

I cannot emphasize enough how valuable it is to **collaborate with a tapping coach.** You will be able to get more specific help with the support of a professional.

The last note I want to give is remember that everything is connected. For example, if you are not getting the money you believe you deserve, you will likely find the sources of that challenge in some apparently unrelated memories. For example, you were the second or third child and ended up with your siblings hand-me-downs or you have heard your parents say many times that "money is filthy." **There are likely multiple roots to this weed-like belief.** Every time you cut out a root, you make the weed weaker until it dies and you can't even remember what it was like to live with this block.

This has been happening to me a lot. I was afraid of so many things that I would need a dictionary to go through all of them. Now, not as much! And I can't even remember how it impacted me. **It seems utterly foreign, because it actually was.**

I hope you are feeling excited. I am very excited for you! **Creating more freedom and reconnecting with one's authentic self is the best feeling in the world** and I am honored to be part of your process. Enjoy and good luck!

Tap when you feel stressed in general or about a situation in particular. Connect to the feelings in your body, the thoughts in your mind, and the overall emotion. Tap lightly with the tip of your fingers on the points mentioned. If you are new to tapping and havening, you can refer to section 1 for a tapping map and more details on tapping.

**Feel free to substitute your own words.*

Eyebrow: Releasing and letting go of all the stress, the anxiety, the resentment, the anger, and the fear.

Side of eye: Releasing and letting go of all the sadness, the worries, the hurt, and the confusion.

Under eye: Releasing and letting go of all the tension in my body, the pressure in my head, heart, and belly.

Collarbone: Releasing and letting go of all the self-defeating words, the self-loathing, and the self-hatred. Releasing and letting go.

Grab your wrist, breathe, and say "Peace."

Put your hands on your heart and take a breath.

Havening with your hands on your face three times, say "Peace," "Safe," and "Calm."

Repeat three times or as necessary.

JOURNALING – HOW ARE YOU FEELING?

What did you notice during this week in your body, mind, and spirit? **What was your first experience with tapping?** Did things come up? Were you surprised? Continue tapping!

How are you feeling with the microdosing regimen? Did you notice any difference? Are you feeling lighter, or more uplifted? What is the assessment of your progress? Often, we will experience a dip. This is our subconscious "fighting back." It is normal. Stick with the microdosing and the clearing.

• • • • •

The objective of **Week 6** is to bring your mojo back.

VISUALIZATION – I MADE IT!

Our strategy here is to continue your microdosing and tapping while adding in visualization. Every morning when you get up and each night before you sleep, **I want you to spend a couple of**

minutes picturing your vision of success as if it's already real. If you want more professional success in your life, see yourself as confident, in the position you desire, and having reached the level of success you aspire to. If it is more zest for life, imagine and feel yourself as light, happy, calm, and enthusiastic throughout a normal day. This visualization should make you feel energized and excited.

Your visualization doesn't have to be perfect; you just have to imagine that your intention is there already. Visualization just means "see it as if it has happened." When you were a kid you were probably day-dreaming quite a bit. That is visualization!

Every morning when you get up and every night before you sleep, I want you to spend a few minutes envisioning your intention as if it's already real.

TAPPING – I MADE IT AND I AM SAFE

This week's tapping session is the continuation of week 5. You will stick with safety-oriented tapping. Now, though, you want to focus on feeling safe, having reached your vision. **You are safe to shine, safe to have big goals, and safe to win.**

Tap the new script of Week 6 every day this week. Feel free to tap several times a day!

> *Before tapping, visualize your success and focus on any discomfort popping up. Maybe you hear your relatives criticizing you, or you see your friends turning their back to you, or you might feel selfish, lonely, or sad.*
>
> *Connect to the feelings in your body, the thoughts in your mind, and the overall emotions. Tap lightly*

with the tip of your fingers on the points mentioned. If you are new to tapping and havening, you can refer to section 1 for a tapping map and more details on tapping.

**Feel free to substitute your own words.*

Eyebrow: Releasing and letting go all of the stress, the anxiety, the resentment, the anger, and the fear.

Side of eye: Releasing and letting go of all the sadness, the worries, the hurt, and the confusion.

Under eye: Releasing and letting go of the tension in my body, the pressure in my head, heart and belly.

Collarbone: Releasing and letting go of the self-defeating words, the self-loathing, and the self-hatred. Releasing and letting go.

Grab your wrist, breathe, say "Peace."

Put your hands on your heart and take a breath.

Havening with your hands on your face three times, say "Peace," "Safe," "Calm."

Repeat three times or as necessary.

JOURNALING – SUCCESSFUL AND CALM

What did you notice this week in your body, mind, and spirit? How are you feeling with the microdosing regimen? What is the assessment of your progress? What shifts are you feeling in your internal state? **Can you now think, visualize, say out loud, or write your intention with a calm mind?** Does it feel possible?

What new ideas are coming up that support your intention? Act on them! If more things come up in terms of memories and beliefs, write them down and tap on them specifically. Stay with it.

BONUS WORK – LEVERAGE YOUR SENSE OF SMELL

Smell and memory are closely linked. Remember La Madeleine from Proust's *In Search of Lost Time*? The author elegantly connected the ability of our senses to bring back memories and emotions. **Let's use your sense of smell to your advantage to deepen the tapping.** Smell essential oils prior to tapping, such as lavender, which is calming. This will help your subconscious associate calmness with lavender. In your day-to-day life, smell lavender when you feel agitated or before a difficult situation. It will calm you down quickly!

How to accelerate your growth.

Key Takeaways – Chapter 7

- If your nervous system has been stuck in **fight-flight-freeze in childhood**, it will stay there, because this is its **default setting.**
- The first goal of this week is to **calm you in absolute terms** when you are not engaged in any specific activity.
- The second goal is **to make you feel safe and calm when you are going after your dreams and fulfilling your potential.**
- Your brain likely **associated shining, being excited, and competition with rejection**.
- Your subconscious is **playing "against you" by trying to protect you.**
- You are **living the shadow of your life** by only half-playing in a mini sandbox. This creates significant **mental anguish**.
- You are in a **tiny simulation**, playing a **weak avatar** created **mindlessly by others.**
- Tapping will **clear up the bugs and change your default modes**.
- Both tapping and microdosing will help you to **calm your nervous system and remove the default settings** of these protection mechanisms.
- Your tapping practice will help you with **uncovering and releasing the limiting beliefs** that are keeping you stuck.
- You will likely **experience physical reactions** (yawning, hiccups, burping, coughing) when tapping. This is normal and good.
- There are likely **multiple roots to this weed-like limiting belief.** Every time you cut a root, you make the weed weaker until it dies and **you can't even remember what it was to live with this block.**

- Creating more freedom and **reconnecting with one's authentic self** is the best feeling in the world.
- **Picture your vision of success** as if it's already real.
- Your visualization doesn't have to be perfect; you just have to **imagine that your intention is there already**.
- You are safe to shine, safe to have big goals, and **safe to win.**
- Can you now think, visualize, say out loud, and write **your intention with a calm mind**?
- You can **use your sense of smell to your advantage** to deepen the tapping.

Chapter 8

Weeks 7–9 – Accelerating the Transformation

The next three weeks are all about **feeling worthy of the success you are looking for.**

You know by now that you have the success you believe you deserve, not the success you actually deserve. **We want you to believe, 100 percent, that your success is completely aligned with who you are.** It is obvious, it is fun, and it is who you are at your core. The situation you are in today is just the reflection of what you were thinking, oozing, being, and doing in the past. This doesn't determine anything when it comes to your future success. It is a launch pad.

By changing how your subconscious sees you and the world, you will impact the level of success you have. We all meet people who were definitely not talented (or at least not as talented as us!), but who had a tremendous level of success. These people were utterly congruent between their thoughts, their actions, their beliefs, their emotions, and their nervous system.

I agree that it is sometimes difficult to look beyond prejudices and unfair advantages. But **how is focusing on others' advantages vis-à-vis yours helping you??** It only reinforces your subconscious beliefs that you are "less than" and not entitled to the same success as others. And then comes the incongruence between what you want and what you believe you deserve deep down. **The more you focus on how disadvantaged and unlucky you are compared to others, the more unworthy you will feel and the less successful you will be.**

Your level of success in this world is directly proportional to your level of self-worth. So we want to increase your level of self-worth. We don't want to make you work like a dog, while you're unconsciously convinced you are not up to par with your desires anyway. That would be a massive waste of resources. First things first: **you need to have a strong intrinsic sense of self-worth.**

You also know by now that your subconscious is always watching, so **focus on what is going in your favor**, what is supporting your success, and how amazingly worthy you are of this intention. Intention and attention are closely connected—use them to your advantage. It is interesting to see how brainwashing and conditioning are always seen as negative processes. But they are just that: a process. You can actually use your brain's excellent ability to be conditioned and brainwashed to your advantage.

In order to be successful, you first need to make space and remove the garbage. To be totally transparent, **you do face an uphill battle when it comes to unconditioning yourself first.**

These programs have been installed in childhood when your brain had no filter and was taking everything at face value. In addition, this buggy software was installed by your caregivers—the people who mattered the most to you—and you gave them a lot of weight. This is the reason I put so much emphasis on clearing and cleaning. You need healthy foundations first before installing brand new floors, walls, and windows. It's the same for our brain.

Each week of the diet is important. The process mindfully builds from one week to the next. We cleared our body, mind, and environment; we increased our sense of safety, even in the face of future success; in the next three weeks, we will increase your sense of self-worth and continue to build new programs for this new, successful YOU.

MICRODOSING – INCREASED FREQUENCY FOR THE NEXT 3 WEEKS

During Weeks 7-9, **we will increase the frequency of psilocybin to 100mg every other day**. Similarly to the previous week, you will connect to your intention and visualize it as having already occurred. Feel the feelings, hear the sounds, smell the perfume, and make it as real as possible. It only takes a few seconds. You are probably already feeling more joyful thanks to the psilocybin and tapping. We want to harness these great changes! They are the first steps to your transformation into more of who you want to be and more of what you want to have. Your subconscious is watching, thinking, "Wow, I might be able to pull that off!" That is great and we want more of that. **We want to recondition your subconscious for success, calm, and safety.**

• • • • •

In **Week 7**, we will focus on a common sticking point in the lives of many: not feeling good enough as we are.

This unfortunate feeling is an epidemic. I am referring to the lack of the good stuff, the self-generated self-worth. Not the self-worth coming from money, looks, possessions, last name, number of followers, and so on. **I'm talking about the sense of being worthy regardless of the external circumstances.** It is almost impossible to really grasp this concept, as our "being" is so untangled with our "having." You can start having a glimpse of this by asking yourself the questions in the journaling exercises: How would I feel if I were suddenly very rich? Do I feel a sense of power, pride, and increased physical height almost? Do you see yourself standing taller? Reversely, how would I feel if I were suddenly very poor? Do I feel a sense of shame, hurt, sadness, and a desire to hide? With perfect self-generated self-worth, these external conditions don't matter; you know you are worthy regardless of the situation.

Of course, we are not looking for perfect intrinsic self-worth here! I am not aiming at becoming the Dalai Lama and I am sure you are not either. What we want, though, is **a level of self-worth that will support your vision, intention, dreams, and goals**. Over time, as your vision expands, you will have to continue to expand your self-worth. But we need to take one step at a time. Right now, let's aim for the next level of self-worth that will create the next level of success for you.

There are many ways to detect that you need more self-worth. In my case, it took me decades to even realize I had low self-worth, which was a huge barrier to my success. I will share my story as I really want you to avoid wasting the same amount of time, energy, and resources I did. Actually, this entire book is about sharing my experience to **make you as successful as possible in the**

minimum amount of time and effort. This is the book I wished I had twenty years ago; my life would have been wildly different and so much more successful.

For as long as I can remember, I have worked very hard to "better myself." When I was a young adult, it was about learning foreign languages, communication, leadership skills, or speed-reading, to only name a few topics. And these were in addition to practicing all the sports you can play, and studying all the books one can read during one's life. There was not a learning program that I would not want to follow. Then, the trainings became different: hypnosis, meditation, tapping, NLP, coaching, and so on. **I had intuitively figured out that "something was off," but I could not pinpoint what it was.** Focusing on what was happening between my two ears seemed like the right thing to focus on. On the surface, this betterment process is very laudable, after all aren't education, hard work, and excellence the keys to success?

The challenge was that all of these initiatives were not really aimed at making me better; **they were aimed at making me "good enough" or " acceptable."** And as you can imagine, feeling "good enough" or "acceptable" is a pretty elusive goal, especially when you have no idea that it is what you are actually chasing. For the longest time, I sincerely believed that I was just intellectually curious and ambitious (which I definitely am) and that the search for betterment was part of the process of being human (which it is, to some degree).

It took me a very long time to realize that the little voice in my head who was constantly criticizing me, putting me down, and judging me was not "right." That I was not constantly a terrible person, a disappointment, or a total shame. When people were referring to self-hatred, or self-loathing, I never for a second thought that I was in that camp. **Of course, I could not accept myself as I was, but, in my mind, it had nothing to do with self-hatred. It was just reality!** Of course, I used to tell myself, it is totally and utterly unacceptable for me not to be perfectly smart, knowledgeable, pretty, kind, fun, and the whole shebang This is just basics. It is not even perfection! Of course, I should be able to speak three languages without a hint of an accent, be a competitive ballroom dancer, excel at tennis, have a super successful career, fit into my sixteen year old selves jeans, and be financially independent. After all, James Bond does it all. It is only normal that I should be doing as much as him, if not better! These were all things I used to tell myself.

I could not see that my deep lack of self-worth was behind this quest for betterment, which in reality, was an unrealistic quest for perfection in the hope of one day being "acceptable."

So let's say that I was pretty far gone in the delusional spectrum of what my minimum standard or "MVP" (Minimum Viable Product in tech lingo) was and that there was no relief in sight for me in this constant quest for the Good Enough Me. The Me I could finally accept, maybe even love, and be proud of (without knowing that self-love and self-worth were really what I was after). In the last few years, though I started seeing through that web of lies and finally come to **the realization that my perspective of what my life should be was deeply flawed**, it had been quite challenging as I was trying to accept my "normality" (no, I am not James Bond and this standard might be unrealistic), my little voice was screaming that I was lazy or settling for mediocrity.

One of the challenges I have been facing my whole life is my neurodivergence, which makes me **very literal and not necessarily great with handling the nuances of "real life."** I had habits that were not "normal" in many areas of my life. For example, my mother, brother, boyfriends, and friends cut my meat until I was twenty years old and I was always traveling with my own food. I was in my twenties the first time I ate a sandwich and in my forties the first time I prepared one (I had no choice. I was at a friend's cottage and was tasked with "making the sandwiches for lunch"). And I am only mentioning a few food-related bizarreries. All of my "habits" were very normal to me, I never looked at myself as "different." My friends and family were used to my idiosyncrasies. I also had learned how to behave in "socially acceptable ways" by watching others and imitating their behaviors, so I was mostly able to fly under the radar. But the "normal" patterns of thoughts and behaviors were not innate to me. This inability to adequately grasp nuances and see through the lies prevented me to see for the longest time that I was not aiming at realistic goals. My radar was not just off it was broken, sending me in directions that were plainly impossible for me to reach. Hence, the massive amount of self-loathing coming from always falling short of my goals. No matter how unrealistic these goals were. From my perspective, my very low value and success rate were just a fair assessment.

Now looking back, I see the signs of my extreme naivete. I used to blush a lot, which was awfully embarrassing in social and professional settings (and also a very visible sign of my extreme shame at being myself). Fifteen years ago, my doctor saw me blushing while I was answering an innocuous question and offered to prescribe betablockers to minimize the inconvenience. When she saw my puzzled look, she said, "Half of Bay Street (the Canadian equivalent of Wall Street or The City) is on this type of medication." She would have known, her office was located in one of the main bank towers and she was the official drug provider of the high-powered executives who impressed me so much at the time. I turned her down and decided I would manage my blushing the hard way by uprooting the causes versus barely managing the symptoms (like James Bond would!). But here was a real-life hint that **human beings deemed successful had "weaknesses,"** but I was not ready to hear it. In my mind, I was the unacceptable problem, not the norm.

However, as I became more and more engaged in my personal and spiritual development, I started having more and more Aha! moments when it came to my very low levels of self-love and self-worth. So much so that my intention before an exhausting and pretty scary experience in a Mexican sweat lodge six years ago was for "high self-generated self-worth." Unfortunately at the time, I still didn't understand that **changes were gradual**. I was expecting to wake up one morning with total and absolute self-love and self-worth. Just like that: Boom! But at least it was a sign that I had realized I needed to make some progress on that front.

Two years ago, during my first psilocybin journey, which was very intense to say the least, one of the main messages I received was related to my self-love and self-worth (or rather lack thereof). And it was pretty graphic. In my altered state of consciousness, I could see a sorcerer-shaman removing snakes, rats, and other "dark" creatures from my body—a pretty clear message targeted at my long-standing and deep self-hatred that was overdue for a clearing. **If I ever wanted to get to the next level, I absolutely needed to get rid of this self-loathing**, finally creating space for self-respect, self-love, self-confidence and self-esteem.

It is of primordial importance that you too feel high self-worth. I had the biggest Aha! moment related to this fact after a great tapping session a year ago. A very clear understanding dawned on me, deep down, like a lightning bolt: **"How could I expect success and money while I am assessing myself as being of low value?"** It is almost laughable when you take a minute to really stay with this message. How could someone who judges, criticizes, and invalidates themselves on a constant basis expect others to behave differently? How could we expect professional success at the level of our potential while being plagued by crippling self-doubt, self-judgment and self-loathing?

It had been such a shock for me to realize that **all of us are in some way or another suffering from low self-love and self-worth, but, at the same time, expecting (or at least hoping) for great success and money**. Intellectually, I had a strong inkling that this was true, but now I *know* it at a cellular level, in my bones. And I want you to really sit with it and understand the implications it has on your life. How much did this low self-worth cost you? How many opportunities have you sabotaged? Where would you be if you had had a solid sense of worthiness?

High Self-Worth =
Potential Realized =
Maximized Success

Low Self-Worth =
Self-Sabotage =
Unrealized Potential =
Crumbs of Success

It really doesn't matter if this low self-worth is coming from Dad, Mom, siblings, schools, church, or aliens. The only thing that matters is that **now, at this minute, you can make a conscious choice** to either continue driving with one foot on the accelerator and one on the brake—meaning working very hard for any success and money, while secretly loathing yourself, or you can decide to **remove your foot from the brake**—meaning releasing the self-judgment, self-criticism, and self-hatred to fully benefit from your entire potential and efforts.

This realization has really transformed the way I look at myself and my goals. Yes, I want the book you are holding in your hands to be commercially successful which requires tremendous amounts of work, *but* **I also choose to believe that I am good enough for this success**. And thus I've removed my foot off the brake.

I could have spent all my time working on my book with my foot 100 percent on the accelerator, (soothing my lack of self-confidence via workaholism at the same time), hoping that my massive efforts combined with my current level of self-worth (foot 80 percent on the brake) would do the trick. But this would only give me 20 percent of the possible results.

Or **I could allocate some time to increase my self-worth and confidence**, freeing some time from my perfectionism, becoming more effective when working on my book (foot 40 percent on the brake) while still allocating significant amount of time to my book (foot 75 percent on the accelerator). This would give me 35 percent of the possible results, while having long-term increased benefits from heightened self-worth. I liked the second math better!

I hope that you have now totally, utterly, and completely convinced yourself of the massive impact that your self-worth has on your life. I also hope that you are 100 percent committed to increasing your self-worth. Whether you have 20 percent, 40 percent, 60 percent, or even 80 percent of your total self-worth, more precisely self-generated self-worth, it doesn't matter. **You will benefit from more intrinsic self-worth regardless.**

Everything you have been doing and will be doing in this book aims at increasing your level of self-worth in the direction of your vision. You will be looking at improving your general sense of worthiness, but you will (and have been) focusing specifically on the self-worth linked with your vision and intention. Of course, I want you to feel high self-worth in all aspects of your life. However, if you are aiming for a promotion, increasing your body-worthiness might not be the most direct way to go. It would be helpful, but not an optimal, nor strategic approach.

Once again, microdosing, tapping, and visualizing will be our winning combo to help you uninstall the faulty software and download state of the art supportive programs.

TAPPING – FEELING WORTHY IN DAILY LIFE

Last week, you visualized yourself in situations of success and tapped away the limiting beliefs as well as the physical and emotional reactions that were not supportive of your success. The goal was to build a sense of safety around being successful. This week, you will visualize yourself in various situations from the most mundane to the most exceptional. **You will tap away the limiting beliefs as well as the physical and emotional reactions that are alerting you that "something is wrong" and needs to be adjusted.** They are helpful. These are the messages that your subconscious is sending you, such as "Who do you think you are?" You can't do that!" and "This is not for people like you." These messages are telling you that something is wrong with you; you are not behaving the way you should; "this is unacceptable and you are not good enough." Bingo! That's the part we need to work on.

I want you to visualize yourself in different situations: social settings, business meetings, with your partner, with your family or friends, speaking on a stage, asking for a raise, receiving a compliment, negotiating, saying no to someone, and so on. Start with what seems to be the most natural to you and then what you know is slightly more uncomfortable. **At some point, you will feel an internal tug of war.** Maybe your stomach will be churning, you will start to blush, or your throat will tighten. **This is an indicator that you feel you do not believe it is okay to be yourself in that situation.** As soon as you feel that discomfort, start tapping. Please note that you might have difficulty feeling: this is not at all uncommon. Do the tapping regardless.

Tap the new script of Week 7 every day this week. As always, feel free to tap several times a day!

> *Before tapping, visualize yourself in different situations, from the most mundane to the most challenging. When you start feeling a tug of war, you are ready for an impactful session of tapping.*
>
> *Connect to the feelings in your body, the thoughts in your mind, and the overall emotion. Tap lightly with the tip of your fingers on the points mentioned. If you are new to tapping and havening, you can refer to section 1 for a tapping map and more details on tapping.*
>
> **Feel free to substitute your own words.*
>
> *Eyebrow: Releasing and letting go of all the stress, the anxiety, the resentment, the anger, and the fear.*
>
> *Side of eye: Releasing and letting go of all the sadness, the worries, the hurt, and the confusion.*
>
> *Under eye: Releasing and letting go of the tension in my body, the pressure in my head, heart, and belly.*
>
> *Collarbone: Releasing and letting go of the self-defeating words, the self-loathing, the self-hatred. Releasing and letting go.*

Grab your wrist, breathe, and say, "Peace."

Put your hands on your heart and take a breath.

Havening with your hands on your face three times, say "Peace," "Safe," "Worthy."

Repeat three times or as necessary.

Repeat this exercise ideally several times each day, until you feel that your physical symptoms of discomfort have greatly diminished (i.e. on a scale of zero to ten, tap until you are consistently below a four). **Many people struggle with the limiting belief that they are not good enough as they are, and it may take time to neutralize this.** Feel free to repeat this tapping for an additional week if you like. Adding one more week will not change anything in your plan in the grand scheme of things, but it can support your success.

JOURNALING – OVERALL INTRINSIC SELF-WORTH

First, let's take a sneak peek at your self-worth. Ask yourself: how would I feel if I were suddenly very rich? Do you feel a sense of power, pride, and increased height almost? Reversely, how would I feel if I were suddenly very poor? Do you feel a sense of shame, hurt, sadness, or a desire to hide? Write down what comes up for you.

Then, I want you to jolt every memory you have of you doing great things, being worthy, any experiences that support your vision. Don't hesitate to embellish them; they are reference points your subconscious will use to remind itself of how great you are. You want to put them front and center so it can access it quickly and easily. **You are leveraging what is called the availability**

bias, which is the human tendency to rely on information that comes readily to the mind when evaluating situations or making decisions.

Last but not least, tapping can be very emotional and it might have been the case for your session. It is a good sign because it means you are releasing pent up stress and negative emotions. **Journal on what came up with the tapping.** What were the physical symptoms? What thoughts and memories came to your mind? Did you feel lighter after tapping? How are you enjoying microdosing, visualizing, and tapping? What progress did you make this week?

• • • • •

During **Week 8**, you will again focus on the misguided belief that you are not enough.

This time, you will get more specific as you zoom in on your intention. **We want to increase your perception that you are worthy of your vision.** This success is totally aligned with who you are. You believe, you ooze, you know that this success is normal. It just is. It is yours. It is in you. It is you. Think about trust fund kids; they never doubt that they will have the money to do what they want to do. Being wealthy is as natural for them as breathing. You want to emulate that sense of entitlement (not everything is bad with feeling entitled!).

You are entitled to your vision. **You are your intention.** The connection between who you know you are authentically and your intention is so congruent that you are convinced deep-down that it can't be otherwise. The sun will rise tomorrow and your intention is yours. That's the spirit. Every little self-doubt, question, or "but," you will tap away. You don't even need to know what they are, where they are coming from, when they appeared, and why. The physical and emotional sensations and thoughts are the signs that some stuff needed to be cleared up (or integrated, depending on which lingo resonates best with you). **As you remove these barriers to success, you naturally get closer to it.**

Many of us actually squirm at the idea of reaching our vision, of having our intention materialize. **We have been so used to struggling and not getting what we want that it is scary to get what we want.** On one hand, we ardently desire to succeed. On the other hand, we don't think we can handle it. Success is so unfamiliar, especially if it comes without pain and difficulties, that we are dubious. There must be a trick. And having low self-worth put us in situations that caused us to doubt that great things could happen to us. We tell ourselves, "who am I to get that great thing?"

The "no pain, no gain" mindset (thank you again hustle culture!) is so ingrained, especially in North America, that we imagine we will have to slay three dragons before getting the prize. And this belief makes everything more difficult. You don't want to turn delusional thinking that with three affirmations and a vision board success will magically appear. I have news for you, it won't, unless you already have the self-worth built up to that level of success. **Without high levels of congruence between your self-worth and your intention, it will be nearly impossible for you to get what you want.** Or you might get it and then you will sabotage yourself as fast as you can say "Will Smith." We want you to build for the long-term, for the forever, a rock-solid self-worth that will bring you rock-solid success that stands the test of time because it is 100 percent *you.*

TAPPING – FEELING WORTHY OF YOUR INTENTION

Visualize and feel situations where your vision of success has been achieved. See yourself as being, looking, and speaking as you would when your vision has materialized. Feelings of discomfort will likely pop up; start tapping and release them.

Tap the new script of Week 8 every day this week. As always, feel free to tap several times a day!

Before tapping, visualize yourself in different situations, from the most mundane to the most challenging. When you start feeling a tug of war, go for it!

Connect to the feelings in your body, the thoughts in your mind, and the overall emotion. Tap lightly with the tip of your fingers on the points mentioned. If you are new to tapping and havening, you can refer to section 1 for a tapping map and more details on tapping.

**Feel free to substitute your own words.*

Eyebrow: Releasing and letting go of all the stress, the anxiety, the resentment, the anger, and the fear.

Side of eye: Releasing and letting go of all the sadness, the worries, the hurt, and the confusion.

Under eye: Releasing and letting of go the tension in my body, the pressure in my head, heart, and belly.

Collarbone: Releasing and letting go of the self-defeating words, the self-loathing, the self-hatred. Releasing and letting go.

Grab your wrist, breathe, and say "Peace."

Put your hands on your heart and take a breath.

Havening with your hands on your face 3 times, say "Peace," "Safe," "Worthy."

Repeat three times or as necessary.

As per week 7, repeat this exercise ideally several times each day, until you feel that your physical symptoms of discomfort have greatly diminished (i.e. on a scale of zero to ten, tap until you are consistently below a four). Please feel free to repeat this week if you believe it will best support your success.

JOURNALING –SELF-WORTH CONGRUENT WITH BEING SUCCESSFUL

This is assessment week! Where are you on the zero to ten scale for the area you were looking to improve? Have other areas improved too? What is your overall score now? What is the percentage of improvement? What benefits have you experienced in terms of performance (both mental and physical), mental wellness, or spirituality? How far do you feel you have come? What did you learn over the last few weeks regarding your limiting patterns and beliefs? **How confident do you feel in your ability to be more successful, more in control of your life, and more able to decide for yourself?** You still have four weeks to go, and you've already made so much progress. Take this time to celebrate that.

You might even experience better physical health, such as less back pain and better digestion. **You must feel more relaxed and present, have more fun with your friends and family, and be overall happier.**

• • • • •

Week 9 is upon you and we will include a different type of tapping!

As you have hopefully noticed, we've tapped away the blocks in the previous weeks, and now we will start turning to the positive by anchoring good feelings with your intention. **It is very important to remove the weeds prior to any attempt at planting new seeds.** Your internal garden will never be totally free of weeds, but you have removed enough of them now that you can plant your new beautiful flowers, fruits, and vegetables with a high probability of a wonderful harvest. I constantly release and integrate weeds.

I was initially frustrated by that process; "Didn't I already remove enough crap?" But the reality is that we don't take one great shower on Monday and then stay away from any personal hygiene activities forever or even for one week. It is the same for our internal state; new and old things pop up, sometimes in a different way, that require our care. Now, I look at this clearing process differently. Every time something comes up, such as limiting belief, self-doubt, or physical discomfort, I know that I am ready to free myself from more blocks and reach for a higher level of success. Look at this process as a spiral that's non-linear, never ending, and always reaching up. **Like a flower looking for the sun, you are unfolding and expanding better without weeds sucking up your nutrients.** I really eat my own dog food; the program you are following is the program I follow. This is why I can tell you that you will have such an upgrade in your life and this is also why I am so happy to be sharing The Microdose Diet with you. I sincerely believe that this regimen makes the world a better place by making all of us more authentic people with higher levels of self-worth and success. **Reaching your potential is an essential component of a life well-lived.**

TAPPING – THE "DREAM YOU" FEELING

This week, you will be **embodying your "Dream You,"** the You who is successful and whose intention has materialized.

You will now use tapping to **anchor the positive feelings** you have been feeling in your body and mind. Visualize yourself moving through a normal day, feeling happy, light, free, and successful. Imagine yourself saying hello and smiling at strangers, totally embodying this new you. It probably starts to feel familiar and good. Once you get that feeling of being light, free, fulfilled, and excited about life, start tapping.

Do the tapping session for week 9 every day, up to several times a week.

> *Before tapping, visualize yourself having manifested your intention. You are successful! When you start feeling the great feelings, go for it!*
>
> *Connect to the feelings in your body, the thoughts in your mind, and the overall emotion. Tap lightly with the tip of your fingers on the points mentioned. If you are new to tapping and havening, you can refer to section 1 for a tapping map and more details on tapping.*
>
> **Feel free to substitute your own words.*
>
> *Eyebrow: I feel great success now*
>
> *Side of eye: It is safe for me to experience great success*

Under eye: I feel great success in every cell of my being

Collarbone: Amplifying my great success now

Grab your wrist, breathe, and say "Peace."

Put your hands on your heart and take a breath.

Havening with your hands on your face three times, say "Peace," "Safe," "Worthy."

Repeat three times or as necessary.

Continue tapping on anything that looks like a limiting belief. You can also tap when you feel amazing to anchor this feeling in your mind and body, reprogramming your nervous system for happy thoughts and a calm body. Continue clearing your physical space of anything that doesn't feel aligned anymore.

JOURNALING – JOYFUL CHANGES

How much more joyful do you feel? Are people around you starting to notice how you have changed, how much lighter you are?

BONUS WORK: MAXIMIZE YOUR TAPPING

The roof of your mouth (soft palate) links to your parasympathetic system via several meridian points. The parasympathetic system calms and focuses the mind. **Before tapping, place the tip of your tongue on the roof of your mouth to benefit from this calm and focus.**

Three benefits of journaling.

Key Takeaways – Chapter 8

- You want to believe 100 percent that **this success is totally aligned with who you are.**
- By changing how your subconscious sees you and the world, **you will impact the level of success you have.**
- The more you focus on how disadvantaged and unlucky you are compared to others, **the more unworthy you will feel and the less successful you will be.**
- Focus on what is going **in your direction.**
- To get what you want, you need to have a **strong intrinsic sense of self-worth**. The sense of being **worthy regardless of the external circumstances.**
- You do face an **uphill battle** when it comes to **unconditioning yourself.**
- Every week of The Microdose Diet is very important and **builds on each previous week.**
- We want to **recondition your subconscious for success**, calm and safety, and develop a level of **self-worth that will support your vision**, intention, dreams, and goals.
- The goal of this program is to make you **as successful as possible** in the minimum amount of time and effort.
- One might not see that their **deep lack of self-worth** is behind this constant quest for betterment, which, in reality, is an unrealistic quest for perfection in the hopes of one day being **"acceptable."**
- It is of primordial importance that you feel high self-worth. **How can you expect success and money** if you are assessing yourself as being of low value?
- All of us are, in some way or another, suffering from low self-love and self-worth, but at the same time, somehow

expecting (or at least hoping) **for great success and money**, while deep-down thinking **we are not worth it**.

- **High Self-Worth = Potential Realized = Maximized Success.**
- **Low Self-Worth = Self-Sabotage = Unrealized Potential = Crumbs of Success.**
- Now, at this minute, you can make a conscious choice to **remove your foot from the brake**.
- I could have spent all my time and energy working on this book, but I deliberately chose to allocate some of these resources to **increase my self-worth and confidence**.
- Everything you have been doing and will be doing with TMD aims at **increasing your level of self-worth in the direction of your vision**.
- Many people struggle with the limiting belief that they are not good enough as they are, and **it may take time to neutralize this**.
- By remembering past success, you are leveraging what is called the **availability bias**, which is the human tendency to rely on information that comes readily to mind when evaluating situations or making decisions.
- We have been so used to struggling and not getting what we want that **it is scary to get what we want**.
- Without **high levels of congruence between your self-worth and your intention**, it will be nearly impossible for you to get what you want.
- It is very important to **remove the weeds prior** to any attempt at planting new seeds.
- Like a flower looking for the sun, **you will unfold and expand better without weeds** sucking up your nutrients.

- **Reaching your potential** is an essential component of a **life well-lived.**
- Before tapping, **place the tip of your tongue on the roof of your mouth** to benefit from this calm and focus.

Chapter 9

Weeks 10–12 – Anchoring and Embodying the Changes

In the next two weeks, you will remove a few more layers that might prevent you from fully manifesting the success you desire: **the resistance to embody your most authentic self and to change**. In your last week of the program, you will amp up the volume and **deeply anchor the "New You" until it's totally aligned with your vision.**

By embodying, as closely as possible, your vision of success from the inside out (clearing the limiting beliefs and emotional wounds) and the outside in (clearing your thoughts, words, space and upgrading them), **you are as close as you can be from becoming the success you desire**.

There is something to be said for the phrase "fake it till you make it" (or "dress for the job you want"); this concept of mimicking your vision of success is certainly a valuable one—as long as feigned confidence doesn't fall into lies and deception, starting with self-deception. Modeling success when having plenty of limiting beliefs, adverse physical sensations, and emotional reactions to your vision of success will not be helpful, on the contrary. **You can fake it successfully only when the big boulders of fear have become small rocks.**

Assessing our blocks and removing them from our default mode in favor of more supporting beliefs is a non-negotiable first step for real, long-lasting success.

Jumping right to affirmations, positive thinking, and "thoughts becoming things" is not appropriate for most of us. It could be for someone who has been raised in a very enlightened environment, but I have yet to meet such lucky individuals!

The Microdose Diet is a stepping stone to absolutely any personal and professional development you want to engage in.

You want to learn a foreign language? Start by removing all the blocks telling you that you are not good at languages.

You want to lose weight? **The first step is to acknowledge and put on the back burner all the resistance you have to become slimmer.** It might sound irrational, but we have so many sophisticated protection mechanisms that what we consciously believe is great for us, will not be what our unconscious believes. In this context, your unconscious mind might remember that you have criticized slim people in the past, that most of your friends and family members are overweight, and that you don't have the financial means to replace your wardrobe. Making the intention to lose weight without first addressing your blocks is a losing value proposition.

You want to be financially independent? This will require more internal than external work. I have no doubt that you are shrugging with that comment, but it is absolutely true. We have more hang-ups when it comes to money than when it comes to sex. **Money represents so much for us, starting with our own self-worth. Accordingly, tremendous amounts of limiting beliefs are happily populating your minds—conscious and unconscious.**

For me, Money = Mother. The perceived criticism, neglect, rejection, lack of love, humiliation, "not good enough," and lack of safety combined with the emotional roller-coaster, deep fear of being scorned, control and scarcity have been rolled up into my relationship with money, the same way it was with my mother as a child. **It had literally become a one-to-one relationship; Money had replaced my mother.** And unfortunately, this was not a very supportive and loving relationship!

Working directly on money internally and externally was bringing me nowhere, until I understood that what **I needed to focus on was my childhood traumas, specifically with my mother**. Suddenly, doors opened and money started coming in (and sticking around).

My point is that **you will likely be focusing on very old events and patterns that might seem totally unrelated** but actually have everything to do with the situation you are now in.

When you looked at your state of affairs nine weeks ago, there were gaps with your ideal scenario, otherwise you would not have picked up this book. The dissatisfaction you have with your current love life, your career, and your finances have absolutely nothing to do with your current love life, your career, and your finances. **They are just old patterns that are playing out over and over again, until you solve them.** And to make things even more complicated, these patterns are likely not related to the same category. Your lousy finances, for example, are likely to be rooted in a perceived lack of love and validation from your caregivers. The goal is not to understand every little event that led you where you are. That would take five lifetimes. You want to understand enough of the dynamics to connect to the feelings they create and release them (or integrate them).

For example, if I tap on money to improve my ability to receive it easily and pleasantly, I just connect to the overall feelings, thoughts, and memories of **feeling rejected, lonely, and not good enough as a kid at home**. And then I tap. You can use the tapping scripts and adjust them if needed. If you remember specific traumas, you can also apply them to tapping. I would strongly recommend to work with a tapping practitioner for traumas with a big T. They are experts at managing such situations. My absolutely fabulous tapping coach, Pam Wright, who inspired the scripts in this book, is world-class and would be a great support to work on your big stumbling blocks.

You have more power to change your circumstances than you think.

Once you realize that by letting go of unconscious patterns and beliefs and replacing them with more supportive ones, you will be able to increase your self-worth and align with the level of success you desire, you will be infinitely closer to achieving your dreams. **The rest you can manage in the physical world with work and smarts.** You will have the right ideas, the motivation, and the ambition necessary to achieve your vision. **The most important step to success is removing your blocks.**

You would never train as a pole vaulter with ankle weights. You would first remove the ankle weights. Well, this is the same rationale. You can change anything in your world, as long as you are convinced consciously and unconsciously that it is safe and positive for you to experience these changes.

Through microdosing and visualization, **you should now be able to quickly connect to your feelings of peace, joy, success, and freedom**. Try summoning this feeling several times during the day, perhaps when you are in the car, taking public transportation, waiting in line, or walking to a meeting. You can even imagine infusing these great feelings and visions of success to the food you eat, the water you drink, and the air you breathe.

MICRODOSING – INCREASED FREQUENCY FOR THE NEXT THREE WEEKS

Now that you have completed nine weeks of your 90 Day Microdose Diet, you are ready to make psilocybin an even more consistent part of your life. **Increase your frequency to 100mg every Monday through Friday.** You know the drill—connect to your intention, visualize, and feel a strong sense of peace, joy, success, and freedom.

GUIDED MEDITATION – I AM MY MOST AUTHENTIC SELF

Week 10 will introduce guided meditation to your practice. The objective is to clear away another layer of resistance to showing up as your most authentic self.

This meditation will help **release personal blocks that are telling you it is not okay to experience more joy, success, and freedom as your most authentic self.** If this brings up anything new for you, please tap through it using the script from Week 5.

I have been trained in many modalities and you will use the combination of the best tools in the guided meditations to **give**

you the best return on your experience. You don't need to know why and how these practices work to get the benefits from them. However, if you are interested, you can visit the bibliography and further explore the topics that most interest you.

If you are combining the book with the online course available at TheMicrodoseDiet.com, please note that, the music in the background is **delta waves allowing you to access deeper levels in your unconscious**. It is better to listen to it with headphones.

Do the guided meditation for week 10 every day. Feel free to use it multiple times a day!

> *Sit comfortably, where you won't be interrupted, and close your eyes.*
>
> *Imagine that you are looking slightly above eye level.*
>
> *Take a deep breath. On the exhale, mentally see and say the number "three" three times.*
>
> *Take another deep breath. On the exhale, mentally see and say the number "two" three times.*
>
> *Take another deep breath. When you exhale, mentally see and say the number "one" three times.*
>
> *Mentally say "Every day in every way I am feeling better, better, and better."*
>
> *To become even more relaxed, count down from ten to one.*
>
> *Now imagine hundreds of white roses of all sizes clearing up your body, mind, spirit, and energy from all the pretending, the masks, and the falseness you had to embody to fit in.*

These roses are removing all the dust at a cellular level, cleaning up all the old programs and conditioning that don't serve you anymore, creating space for authentic success.

When you feel that the roses have removed everything ready to be cleared at this point, see the roses fly away and disappear into space.

Now imagine a beautiful golden light coming from far away in the universe. This beautiful light represents your most authentic self and success. It flows from the top of your head, to your brain, your eyes, your ears, your throat, your shoulders, your arms, your hands, your lungs, your heart, your liver, your stomach, your kidneys, your intestines, your reproductive organs, your legs, and your feet. Your blood, skin, cells, hair, nails, teeth, organs, bones, muscles, nerves, every fiber of your body is bathed in this beautiful golden light.

The light forms a beautiful bubble around you.

You feel at peace, you feel worthy, you feel deserving of your success, you can be who you want to be authentically, you can do what you want to do authentically.

Enjoy how amazing it feels to be okay exactly as you are. Feel the compassion, the love, the pride for your authentic self and everything it had to let go of to survive.

Thank the golden light and thank yourself for doing this process and supporting yourself.

Slowly move your fingers and toes, take a deep breath, stretch and open your eyes.

This process can be emotional. **When we realize how much we went through, especially as a young kid, strong physical sensations and emotions can pop up.** Stay with them and jump to our first tapping session. You can substitute some words to become more aligned with your specific situation.

As mentioned previously, don't hesitate hiring a tapping coach to work on specific memories or challenges you've identified.

I became very skilled at using tapping to free myself of automatic responses that were no longer helpful. The guilt and shame of not being enough was one of my big emotional wounds and would rear its "ugly head" constantly. I have been able to greatly loosen its grip on me. I have no doubt that as I continue growing in my life, it will come back in another shape to be cleared away again. **But the more I clear it, the weaker it gets, and the more I become aware of its impact on me.**

JOURNALING – BEING MORE AUTHENTIC

Do you feel any difference with this new microdosing regimen?

How easy is it to call those feelings of happiness and light during the day? Do you catch yourself smiling more, laughing more, and having more ideas?

Review your energy map. **Are there any adjustments you want to make to the people, places, and situations to augment your new feelings of joy, success, and freedom?**

How did you enjoy the guided meditation? Did you have moments of clarity or memories coming up? What does it mean for you to be more authentic? Do you have an image you could embody?

• • • • •

During **Week 11**, it's time to get utterly comfortable with change.

You have been doing fabulous. **You have cleared so much in so many areas of your life.** You can really pat yourself on the back. This is no small feat and you are doing it! Remember that it is an inside job, the more convinced—consciously and subconsciously—you become of deserving success, the more you will be able to not only take the right actions, but also to keep this success for the long haul. Bye-bye boom and bust cycles. Self-sabotage will soon be a thing of the past for you.

GUIDED MEDITATION – I LOVE CHANGE!

In this week's guided meditation, **you will uninstall any negative beliefs still lurking regarding change** and you will upgrade your unconscious mind to a new message that change is great, safe, easy, fast, fun, and beneficial. By the end of the week, you'll be saying "I love change!"

Do the guided meditation for week 11 every day. Feel free to use it multiple times a day!

> *Sit comfortably where you won't be interrupted and close your eyes.*
>
> *Imagine that you are looking slightly above eye level.*
>
> *Take a deep breath. One the exhale, mentally see and say the number "three" three times.*
>
> *Take another deep breath. On the exhale, mentally see and say the number "two" three times.*

Take another deep breath. When you exhale, mentally see and say the number "one" three times.

Mentally say "Every day in every way I am feeling better, better, and better."

To become even more relaxed, count down from ten to one.

Now imagine hundreds of white roses of all sizes clearing up your body, mind, spirit, and energy from all the memories of past failures, others' criticisms, rejections for trying something new, and the fear of being seen and heard.

These roses are removing all the dust at a cellular level, cleaning up all the old programs and conditioning that don't serve you anymore, creating space for successful happy change.

When you feel that the roses have removed everything ready to be cleared at this point, see the roses fly away and disappear into space.

Now imagine a beautiful golden light coming from far away in the universe. This beautiful light represents success, fun, and a happy change. It comes from the top of your head to your brain, your eyes, your ears, your throat, your shoulders, your arms, your hands, your lungs, your heart, your liver, your stomach, your kidneys, your intestines, your reproductive organs, your legs, and your feet. Your blood, skin, cells, hair, nails, teeth, organs, bones, muscles, nerves, every fiber of your body is bathed in this beautiful golden light.

The light forms a beautiful bubble around you.

You feel at peace, you feel worthy, you feel capable of handling change, you feel excited about change, you know that change will bring you great authentic success.

Enjoy how amazing it feels to be okay doing something different, something aligned with your dreams. Enjoy how great it feels to be different and be successful in doing so. Enjoy the feeling of being aligned with your most authentic desires and that change is just the process of getting there.

Thank the golden light, thank yourself for doing this process and supporting yourself.

Slowly move your fingers and toes, take a deep breath, and stretch and open your eyes.

JOURNALING – I LOVE CHANGE

How do you feel about change now? Do you feel safer and more excited? Are you convinced that change is fast, easy, and positive for you? **What ideas have been sparked with regard to the changes you would like to create?** What areas of your life are you the most excited to change? What small change can you make this week? **What is one thing you could change or try every month for the next twelve months?**

• • • • •

It's time for our final week: **Week 12**! This is very exciting, even though I know that you have already started feeling so much better over the last few weeks. I know from experience that **ideas, inspired actions, calm, joy, and hope are now part of your daily life and have been propelling you in the direction of your long-term authentic success.**

You now have an opportunity to **deeply anchor your feeling of excitement for life and success.** Enjoy your last week of microdosing with even deeper and clearer feelings of success, excitement, and happiness. Visualize and tap on being the kickass person you are.

Do the visualization and tapping session for week 12 every day, and, as always, feel free to use it multiple times a day!

TAPPING – THE "SUCCESS IS MINE" FEELING

This week, you will be embodying the "Success Is Mine" feeling. Ramping up these emotions, thoughts, and physical sensations.

You will now use tapping to **anchor the positive feelings you have been feeling to your body and mind.** Visualize yourself celebrating your achievements, throwing a party, having a discussion with your friends and family members about how delighted you are to be successful. See yourself with your hands in the air, arms pumping, screaming for joy, pride and excitement. Really psych yourself up!

Do the tapping session for week 12 every day, up to several times a week.

> *Before tapping, visualize yourself celebrating your great success. Feel it! You did it! This is amazing! You fully deserve it, you are so happy and at the same time not surprised at all. This is yours, this is all yours.*

Connect to the feelings in your body, the thoughts in your mind, and the overall emotion. Tap lightly with the tip of your fingers on the points mentioned. If you are new to tapping and havening, you can refer to section 1 for a tapping map and more details on tapping.

**Feel free to substitute your own words.*

Eyebrow: I did it!

Side of eye: I am so happy!

Under eye: This is amazing! I am amazing!

Collarbone: This success is mine and I love it!

Grab your wrist, breathe, and say "Success."

Put your hands on your heart and take a breath.

Havening with your hands on your face three times, say "Successful," "Happy," "Worthy."

Repeat three times or as necessary.

I encourage you to tap as often as you can. It will take you barely a couple of minutes.

If you can't tap, imagine tapping; it works fabulously well. Our brain can't tell the difference between imagination and action, so let's trick it—after all, it has been tricking us enough! I "mind-tap" in bed, before sleeping, or if I wake up during the night. I am also one of those people who tap while walking. If you don't feel like doing that (which I can understand!) just mind-tap while having a walk, or visualize when you are taking the subway or in line at a coffee shop. **You can make a massive difference in your life by**

integrating these tools in your day-to-day life. You don't even have to stop what you are doing. **When engaging in mundane tasks, elevate them with mind-tapping and visualization.**

JOURNALING – I DID IT!

How excited are you about your life and being you? How happy are you? **What are the new projects you want to start?** How confident are you that success is yours?

BONUS WORK – DEEPEN AND TRIGGER THE "SUCCESSFUL YOU" STATE

You can easily anchor and trigger states and behaviors (think of Pavlov's dog) by using a movement of your fingers. When you visualize and feel great about the New You, put your three first fingers together (thumb, index, and middle fingers) and take a deep breath through your nose, as if you were inhaling this picture. Release the fingers, the breath, and the vision. When you want to recall this state, put your three first fingers together. The more you do it, the more ingrained it becomes.

CONGRATULATIONS!

This is the end of the program. Well Done!

I want to commend you for giving yourself the opportunity to transform your life for the better. This program has required you to learn new information, acquire new skills, and more importantly, to question everything about the way you live your life and about who you really are. These are not easy tasks! **Your perspective has started to shift and you probably**

understand better the importance of your internal state and of your level of self-worth in your external success.

Every time you want to bring your life to the next level, come back to this plan. You can follow it every year. Every time you do so, you go deeper and get lighter.

Keep noticing how amazing you are doing, how great you are feeling, how much more attractive you are to others, and how much fun you are having. **Staying present in your life is paramount to keeping this feeling of awe, ooze, and great vibes.**

I have no doubt that people around you will notice how much brighter you shine. **Talk to your dear ones about this plan, lend them this book, or even better, give them a fresh copy!**

Become an ambassador of The Microdose Diet and spread the word that **there is MORE to life and that you are now getting more out of it**. The larger the number of people living their potential, the greater the world will become. By working on yourself, you are supporting the world to become a better place. **Thank You.**

Stop honking, start thinking; our choices can have disproportionate impacts on our lives and others'.

Key Takeaways - Chapter 9

- You will start by **removing the resistance to embodying your most authentic self** and to deeply anchor the **"New You"** which is now totally aligned with your vision.
- You can fake it successfully **only when** the big boulders of fear have become small rocks.
- Jumping right to affirmations, positive thinking, and "thoughts becoming things" is **not appropriate for most of us.**
- **The Microdose Diet is a stepping stone** to absolutely any personal and professional development you want to engage in.
- The first step is to acknowledge and put on the back burner all the **resistance you have to becoming successful.**
- **Money represents so much for us, starting with our own self-worth. Accordingly, tremendous amounts of limiting beliefs are happily populating your minds—conscious and unconscious.**
- For me **Money = Mother**. It has literally been a one-to-one relationship; money had replaced my mother.
- Working directly on **money** internally and externally was bringing me nowhere, until I understood that what I needed to focus on was my **childhood traumas**, specifically with my mother.
- If I tap on money to improve my ability to receive it easily and pleasantly, I just connect to the overall feelings, thoughts, and memories of **feeling rejected, lonely, and not good enough as a kid at home**.

- To **reach your potential and become successful**, you will likely have to focus on very **old events and release patterns that might seem totally unrelated.**
- You have **more power to change your circumstances** than you think.
- The most important step to success is **removing your blocks.** The rest you can manage in the physical world with hard work; it's no longer as complicated.
- Increase your microdosing frequency to **100mg every Monday through Friday.**
- You will use the combination of the best tools in the guided meditations to give you the **best return** on your experience in order to release the personal blocks that are telling you it is not okay to experience more joy, success, and freedom as your most authentic self.
- When we realize how much we went through, especially as a young kid, **strong physical sensations and emotions can pop up.**
- The more I clear the guilt and shame of not being enough, **the weaker it gets**, and the more aware I become of its impact on me.
- Are there any **adjustments** you want to make to the people, places, and situations in your energy map to augment your new feelings of joy, success, and freedom?
- You have **cleared so much in so many areas** of your life. Congratulations!
- You will uninstall any negative beliefs still lurking **regarding change** and you will upgrade your unconscious mind to a new message that **change is great and beneficial.**
- What is one thing you could **change or try** every month for the next twelve months?

- You will deeply **anchor your feelings of excitement for life and success.**
- When engaging in mundane tasks, elevate them with **mind-tapping and visualization.**
- I want to commend you for giving yourself the opportunity **to transform your life.**
- Your perspective has started **to shift** and you probably understand better the importance of your **internal state and of your level of self-worth** in your external success.
- Every time you want to bring your life to the next level, **come back to this plan.**
- **Staying present** in your life is paramount to keeping this feeling of awe, ooze, and great vibes.
- Talk to your dear ones about this plan, lend them this book, or even better, **give them a fresh copy**!
- Become an ambassador of The Microdose Diet and spread the word that **there is MORE to life and that you are now getting more out of it**.

Chapter 10

Maintenance Plan

Once you have finished your ninety-day plan, take a step back to thank yourself for making the effort to rewire your brain and push beyond the limitations you thought existed. Congratulate yourself on learning about the amazing benefits of psychedelics and of alternative medicines for personal transformation. **Through this program, you have unlocked new possibilities for your life**: in your relationships, career, health, and overall sense of joy.

So much more will unfold in the coming years when it comes to the psychedelic industry, such as the development of new psychedelic-based treatments that actually cure mental diseases, widespread legalization of psychedelics and the development of new psychedelic-based supplements, to name only a few of the changes that will drastically improve our lives. Make the most of them.

Based on the success you will experience with this program, **you will likely want more**. This is fabulous, that is what life is about.

First, as I mentioned, I will publish new books **with specific topics covering money, career, but also weight loss, relationships, and health**. This will help you go even deeper into the areas you wish to improve (or continue improving).

Second, **for each level of deconditioning and deprogramming, your subconscious and conscious minds are becoming more and more convinced of your high self-worth**. Consequently, **you are aligning yourself with higher and higher levels of success**, having cleared self-limiting beliefs and self-sabotaging patterns. However, every time you are jumping into a new level (similarly to a video game), new "stuff" needs to be cleared up. It is not smooth sailing to be constantly growing. You are better off, though, being on your front foot , and deciding for yourself that you want to continue to disrupt yourself, versus being disrupted by external circumstances forcing you to grow, usually with not-so-nice events. If you are able to see the gift in this constant delayering that is bringing you closer to your authentic self and to achieving your potential, you will actually enjoy the process. I now do, despite fighting it with all my might initially.

The levels I am referring to are called consciousness by some. It doesn't really matter what sticker you put on it. What matters is the realization that they exist and that your goal is to climb them at your speed. Me being me, I am constantly deprogramming and reconditioning myself to move up. I learned a few things along the way. These levels follow an exponential function; the higher you go, the higher the next step (meaning the more challenging the program is to uninstall) and the higher the impact too. It's **more difficult work, but it's more rewarding**.

There is also a time delay between who you become internally and when the external reality aligns with this new level of you. Meaning, the outside circumstances are always one step behind. Impatience being my second name, and I assume most people's second name, this can turn out to be challenging. I have noticed very fast alignments in some areas and glacial pace alignments in others. I now know that bigger opportunities are constantly coming so I am more relaxed and continue, unfazed, my internal delayering and external actions.

Where I stand today compared to where I was not long ago is a great example. I found a literary agent (or rather he found me), I formalized The Microdose Diet, I wrote this book, I signed a deal with a publisher, and I have been speaking about the benefits of alternative medicines for success across North America. Twelve months prior, I could not find a job despite tremendous efforts in doing so, my advisory business was in the shitter, and I had no prospects in sight. This is quite a change of reality in twelve months. And I expect my next twelve months to be even more spectacular in terms of accomplishments. Of course, in the last twelve months, I did put forward efforts to put this book together and seduce audiences, but no more effort than when I was stuck and unsuccessful. **As I increased my authentic self-worth, better opportunities showed up. I still had to grab them, but they showed up first!**

When it comes to your process, you will see similarities but also differences based on your starting point. Maybe I was at level twenty-two last year while you are at level twelve or thirty-two today. But the concept stays the same.

The best maintenance I would recommend to some is to integrate for the length of the program and then start again. So ninety days in, ninety days out. Because I have been on it for quite some time, and am extremely motivated, I never stop; I am constantly clearing and integrating. That works for me, but it might be a bit intense for most!

Subscribe to my newsletter to get more insights and stay in touch.

Key Takeaways - Chapter 10

- Through this program, **you have unlocked new possibilities for your life**: in your relationships, career, health, and overall sense of joy.
- So much more will unfold in the coming years when it comes to the psychedelic industry. **Make the most of them.**
- Based on the success you will experience with this program, **you will likely want more.**
- **I will publish new books with specific topics** covering money, career, but also weight loss, relationships and health.
- For each level of deconditioning and deprogramming, your subconscious and conscious minds are becoming **more and more convinced of your high self-worth**. Consequently, you are aligning yourself with **higher and higher levels of success.**
- The higher the level of consciousness, **the more difficult the work, and the bigger the reward**.
- There is also **a time delay** between who you become internally and when the external reality aligns with this new level of you.
- As I increased my authentic self-worth, better opportunities showed up. **I still had to grab them**, but they showed up first!
- When it comes to your process, **you will see similarities but also differences** based on your starting point.
- The best maintenance I would recommend to most is to **integrate for the length of the program and then go again at it, start again**. So ninety days in, ninety days out.

Chapter 11

Conclusion

You now have all the tools, neatly bundled in one easy-to-follow protocol, for you to get the success you deserve. I want to leave you with the centering theme of this book: **in life, we don't get what we deserve, we get what we believe we deserve.**

Make sure your beliefs, emotions, nervous system, thoughts, words, and actions are coherent with the vision you have for yourself and your life. Everything that is incongruent needs to take a back seat and become a tertiary program. **Your default programs will now be aligned with your intention of success.**

This requires constant attention. The reward is worth the efforts. Would you rather be stuck in your old patterns? What is the point of staying on the merry-go-round of conditioning? Living a life framed by old superstitions, traumas, lies, misunderstandings, and habits?

You deserve more than that!

When it comes to alternative medicines, thanks to the push for a **new approach to health management** focused on prevention, promotion, and patient-controlled processes, so much more will unfold in the coming years.

> **"Emancipate yourselves from mental slavery, none but ourselves can free our minds."**
> **–Bob Marley**

This will allow all of us to be **more and more empowered**, in charge of our health and wellness, and freer from an outdated healthcare system that's more focused on illness than health— and that doesn't always have our best interests in mind.

The psychedelic industry in particular will see tremendous progress that will **drastically improve our lives**.

I commend you for benefitting from centuries of anecdotal and scientific research to make the most out of your life. **I'm wishing you a lot of success and I thank you for becoming an ambassador of this program with your friends and relatives.**

Follow me on IG and get behind the scenes' perspective.

Your 90 Day Diet Curriculum

This twelve-week journey combines some of the most powerful medicines—microdosing psilocybin, tapping, havening, journaling, visualizing, and guided meditation—in an easy and simple regimen to create life-changing results. We strategically integrate them to rewire the brain and calm the body, resulting in a decrease in stress and an increase in success and happiness. You can also go to themicrodosediet.com to learn more and register for the online journey.

WEEK 1 – ASSESS YOUR CURRENT STATE AND CLEAR YOUR BODY

Assess ten areas of your life and rank yourself to understand where you're aligned or not, and what's holding you back. Start clearing your body.

WEEK 2 – MAP YOUR ENERGY AND CLEAR YOUR SPACE

Identify where you are allocating your time and energy (people, places, and activities) and identify how much joy this creates. Start clearing your space.

WEEK 3 – CLARIFY YOUR VISION OF SUCCESS

Set an intention for your journey and clarify what it means to feel more fun, joy, and success in your life.

WEEK 4 – LAUNCH INTO FLOW & AWARENESS + INTRODUCING PSILOCYBIN

Get a better picture of what's getting in your way while bringing in more calm, flow, and awareness.

WEEK 5 – CLEAR LIMITING BELIEFS + INTRODUCING TAPPING

Calm your nervous system and clear out the boulders preventing you from living your most authentic life.

WEEK 6 – BRING YOUR MOJO BACK

Start envisioning your intention with tapping and visualization and start feeling safe to shine, win, and have big goals.

WEEK 7 – REPROGRAM YOUR BODY AND MIND – INTRODUCING VISUALIZATION

Reprogram your mind and body and find comfort and growth in difficult or uncomfortable situations.

WEEK 8 – ANCHOR YOUR BODY IN SELF-LOVE & SUCCESS

Tap away the misguided belief that you're not enough and recognize that your mind is playing tricks on you and that you are enough.

WEEK 9 – EMBODY YOUR DREAM YOU

Anchor the positive feelings you've been feeling to your mind and body, making them familiar and safe.

WEEK 10 – CLEAR THE RESISTANCE

Release personal traumas and resistance to connect with your inner peace.

WEEK 11 – NAVIGATE CHANGE

Understand change and recognize that it's good for you. Find comfort and familiarity in change with a strong sense of freedom and peace.

WEEK 12 –VISUALIZE GROWTH

Visualize the kick-ass person you are and enjoy deeper and clearer feelings of success, excitement, and happiness.

Tapping and Guided Meditation Scripts

WEEK 5 - CALMING DOWN AND FEELING SAFE

Tap when you feel stressed in general or about a situation in particular. Connect to the feelings in your body, the thoughts in your mind, and the overall emotion. Tap lightly with the tip of your fingers on the points mentioned. If you are new to tapping and havening, you can refer to section 1 for a tapping map and more details on tapping.

*Feel free to substitute your own words.

Eyebrow: Releasing and letting go of all the stress, the anxiety, the resentment, the anger, and the fear.

Side of eye: Releasing and letting go all the sadness, the worries, the hurt, and the confusion.

Under eye: Releasing and letting go of the tension in my body, the pressure in my head, heart, and belly.

Collarbone: Releasing and letting go of the self-defeating words, the self-loathing, and the self-hatred. Releasing and letting go.

Grab your wrist, breathe, and say "Peace."

Put your hands on your heart and take a breath.

Havening with your hands on your face three times, say "Peace," "Safe," and "Calm."

Repeat three times or as necessary.

WEEK 6 - FEELING SAFE, HAVING MADE IT

Before tapping, visualize your success and focus on any discomfort popping up. Maybe you hear your relatives criticizing you, or you see your friends turning their back to you, or you might feel selfish, lonely, or sad.

Connect to the feelings in your body, the thoughts in your mind, and the overall emotions. Tap lightly with the tip of your fingers on the points mentioned. If you are new to tapping and havening, you can refer to section 1 for a tapping map and more details on tapping.

*Feel free to substitute your own words.

Eyebrow: Releasing and letting go all of the stress, the anxiety, the resentment, the anger, and the fear.

Side of eye: Releasing and letting go of all the sadness, the worries, the hurt, and the confusion.

Under eye: Releasing and letting go of the tension in the body, the pressure in your head, heart, and belly.

Collarbone: Releasing and letting go of the self-defeating words, the self-loathing, and the self-hatred. Releasing and letting go.

Grab your wrist, breathe, say "Peace."

Put your hands on your heart and take a breath.

Havening with your hands on your face three times, say "Peace," "Safe," "Calm."

Repeat three times or as necessary.

WEEK 7 - FEELING WORTHY IN DAILY LIFE

Before tapping, visualize yourself with your intention having manifested. People are looking at you. They are talking about you. When you start feeling a tug of war, you are ready for an impactful session of tapping.

Connect to the feelings in your body, the thoughts in your mind, and the overall emotion. Tap lightly with the tip of your fingers on the points mentioned. If you are new to tapping, you can refer to section 1 for a tapping map and more details on tapping.

*Feel free to substitute your own words.

Eyebrow: Releasing and letting go of all the stress, the anxiety, the resentment, the anger, and the fear.

Side of eye: Releasing and letting go of all the sadness, the worries, the hurt, and the confusion.

Under eye: Releasing and letting go of the tension in the body, the pressure in the head, heart, and belly.

Collarbone: Releasing and letting go of the self-defeating words, the self-loathing, the self-hatred. Releasing and letting go.

Grab your wrist, breathe, and say, "Peace."

Put your hands on your heart and take a breath.

Havening with your hands on your face three times, say "Peace," "Safe," "Worthy."

Repeat three times or as necessary.

WEEK 8 – FEELING WORTHY OF YOUR INTENTION

Before tapping, visualize yourself with your intention having manifested. People are looking at you. They are talking about you. When you start feeling a tug of war, start tapping.

Connect to the feelings in your body, the thoughts in your mind, and the overall emotion. Tap lightly with the tip of your fingers on the points mentioned. If you are new to tapping, you can refer to section 1 for a tapping map and more details on tapping.

*Feel free to substitute your own words.

Eyebrow: Releasing and letting go of all the stress, the anxiety, the resentment, the anger, and the fear.

Side of eye: Releasing and letting go of all the sadness, the worries, the hurt, and the confusion.

Under eye: Releasing and letting of go this tension in the body, this pression in the head, heart, and belly.

Collarbone: Releasing and letting go of the self-defeating words, the self-loathing, the self-hatred. Releasing and letting go.

Grab your wrist, breathe, and say "Peace."

Put your hands on your heart and take a breath.

Havening with your hands on your face 3 times, say "Peace," "Safe," "Worthy."

Repeat three times or as necessary.

WEEK 9 – THE "DREAM YOU" FEELING

Before tapping, visualize yourself having manifested your intention. You are successful! When you start feeling the great feelings, go for it!

Connect to the feelings in your body, the thoughts in your mind, and the overall emotion. Tap lightly with the tip of your fingers on the points mentioned. If you are new to tapping, you can refer to section 1 for a tapping map and more details on tapping.

*Feel free to substitute your own words.

Eyebrow: I feel great success now

Side of eye: It is safe for me to experience great success

Under eye: I feel great success in every cell of my being

Collarbone: Amplifying my great success now

Grab your wrist, breathe, and say "Peace."

Put your hands on your heart and take a breath.

Havening with your hands on your face three times, say "Peace," "Safe," "Worthy."

Repeat three times or as necessary.

WEEK 10 – I AM MY MOST AUTHENTIC SELF

Sit comfortably, where you won't be interrupted, and close your eyes.

Imagine that you are looking slightly above eye level.

Take a deep breath. On the exhale, mentally see and say the number "three" three times.

Take another deep breath. On the exhale, mentally see and say the number "two" three times.

Take another deep breath. When you exhale, mentally see and say the number "one" three times.

Mentally say "Every day in every way I am feeling better, better, and better."

To become even more relaxed, countdown from ten to one.

Now imagine hundreds of white roses of all sizes clearing up your body, mind, spirit, and energy from all the pretending, the masks, and the falseness you had to embody to fit in.

These roses are removing all the dust at a cellular level, cleaning up all the old programs and conditioning that don't serve you anymore, creating space for authentic success.

When you feel that the roses have removed everything ready to be cleared at this point, see the roses fly away and disappear into space.

Now imagine a beautiful golden light coming from far away in the universe. This beautiful light represents your most authentic self and success. It flows from the top of your head, to your brain, your eyes, your ears, your throat, your shoulders, your arms, your hands, your lungs, your heart, your liver, your stomach, your kidneys, your intestines, your reproductive organs, your legs, and your feet. Your blood, skin, cells, hair, nails, teeth, organs, bones, muscles, nerves, every fiber of your body is bathed in this beautiful golden light.

The light forms a beautiful bubble around you.

You feel at peace, you feel worthy, you feel deserving of your success, you can be who you want to be authentically, you can do what you want to do authentically.

Enjoy how amazing it feels to be okay exactly as you are. Feel the compassion, the love, the pride for your authentic self and everything it had to let go of to survive.

Thank the golden light and thank yourself for doing this process and supporting yourself.

Slowly move your fingers and toes, take a deep breath, and stretch and open your eyes.

WEEK 11 – I LOVE CHANGE

Sit comfortably where you won't be interrupted and close your eyes.

Imagine that you are looking slightly above eye level.

Take a deep breath. On the exhale, mentally see and say the number "three" three times.

Take another deep breath. On the exhale, mentally see and say the number "two" three times.

Take another deep breath. When you exhale, mentally see and say the number "one" three times.

Mentally say "Every day in every way I am feeling better, better, and better."

To become even more relaxed, countdown from ten to one.

Now imagine hundreds of white roses of all sizes clearing up your body, mind, spirit, and energy from all the memories of past failures, others' criticisms, and rejections for trying something new, and the fear of being seen and heard.

These roses are removing all the dust at a cellular level, cleaning up all the old programs and conditioning that don't serve you anymore, creating space for successful happy change.

When you feel that the roses have removed everything ready to be cleared at this point, see the roses fly away and disappear into space.

Now imagine a beautiful golden light coming from far away in the universe. This beautiful light represents success, fun, and a happy change. It comes from the top of your head to your brain, your eyes, your ears, your throat, your shoulders, your arms, your hands, your lungs, your heart, your liver, your stomach, your kidneys, your intestines, your reproductive organs, your legs, and your feet. Your blood, skin, cells, hair, nails, teeth, organs, bones, muscles, nerves, every fiber of your body is bathed in this beautiful golden light.

The light forms a beautiful bubble around you.

You feel at peace, you feel worthy, you feel capable of handling change, you feel excited about change, you know that change will bring you great authentic success.

Enjoy how amazing it feels to be okay doing something different, something aligned with your dreams. Enjoy how great it feels to be different and be successful in doing so. Enjoy the feeling of being aligned with your most authentic desires and that change is just the process of getting there.

Thank the golden light, thank yourself for doing this process and supporting yourself.

Slowly move your fingers and toes, take a deep breath, and stretch and open your eyes.

WEEK 12 – SUCCESS IS MINE

Before tapping, visualize yourself celebrating your great success. Feel it! You did it! This is amazing! You fully deserve it, you are so happy and at the same time not surprised at all. This is yours, this is all yours.

Connect to the feelings in your body, the thoughts in your mind, and the overall emotion. Tap lightly with the tip of your fingers on the points mentioned. If you are new to tapping, you can refer to section 1 for a tapping map and more details on tapping.

*Feel free to substitute your own words.

Eyebrow: I did it!

Side of eye: I am so happy!

Under eye: This is amazing! I am amazing!

Collarbone: This success is mine and I love it!

Grab your wrist, breathe, and say "Success."

Put your hands on your heart and take a breath.

Havening with your hands on your face three times, say "Successful," "Happy," "Worthy."

Repeat three times or as necessary.

Endnotes

1 Freud, Sigmund, and G. Stanley Hall. *A General Introduction to Psychoanalysis.* Thompson Dickerson Books, 2013.

2 Wolinsky, H., *Bioethics for the World,* 2006, *EMBO Reports,* 7(4), 354–358. https://doi.org/10.1038/sj.embor.7400670

3 Gabor Maté with Daniel Maté, *The Myth of Normal,* Avery, September 13, 2022.

4 "NCI Dictionary of Cancer Terms," *National Cancer Institute,* https://www.cancer.gov/publications/dictionaries/cancer-terms/def/psychoactive-substance

5 *Drug Addiction and Drug Abuse,* 1990, Jaffe JH, *The Pharmacological Basis of Therapeutics* 8: 522–573.

6 David E. Nichols, "Psychedelics," *Pharmacological Reviews,* U.S. National Library of Medicine, April, 2016, https://www.ncbi.nlm.nih.gov/pmc/articles/PMC4813425/

7 Ibid.

8 "Drug War Stats," *Drug Policy Alliance*, August 2, 2023, https://drugpolicy.org/issues/drug-war-statistics

9 "Psilocybin and Magic Mushrooms," *Medical News Today*, MediLexicon International, https://www.medicalnewstoday.com/articles/308850#what-is-psilocybin

10 Ruairi J Mackenzie, "An Introduction to Five Psychedelics; Psilocybin, DMT, LSD, MDMA and Ketamine," November 16, 2021, https://www.technologynetworks.com/neuroscience/articles/an-introduction-to-five-psychedelics-psilocybin-dmt-lsd-mdma-and-ketamine-355897

11 James Stephen, "Harvard Psilocybin Project: A Retrospective on Psychedelics," *Truffle Report*, September 25, 2021, https://truffle.report/the-harvard-psilocybin-project-a-retrospective/

12 Kathleen Davis, FNP, "What Are Magic Mushrooms and Psilocybin?," March 14, 2023, *Medical News Today*, https://www.medicalnewstoday.com/articles/308850#risks

13 Mason Marks, "A Strategy for Rescheduling Psilocybin," *Scientific American*, 2021, https://www.scientificamerican.com/article/a-strategy-for-rescheduling-psilocybin/

14 A.J. Herrington, "VA Studying Psychedelics as Mental Health Treatment for Veterans," June 24, 2022, https://www.forbes.com/sites/ajherrington/2022/06/24/va-studying-psychedelics-as-mental-health-treatment-for-veterans/?sh=1937a9796c0d

15 Kirsten Grind, Katherine Bindley, "Magic Mushrooms. LSD. Ketamine. The Drugs That Power Silicon Valley," *The Wall Street Journal*, 2023, https://www.wsj.com/articles/silicon-valley-microdosing-ketamine-lsd-magic-mushrooms-d381e214

16 "Magic Mushrooms as Medicine," *ADF*, March 7, 2023, https://adf.org.au/insights/magic-mushrooms-medicine/#:~:text=We've%20learned%20psilocybin%20can,that%20last%20for%20several%20months.&text=It%20

also%20appears%20to%20be,for%20nicotine%20and%20alcohol%20dependence.

17 Avi Wolfman-Arent, "A 1960s State Official Claimed PA. College Students Took LSD and Went Blind — and Newspapers Believed Him," *Billy Penn at WHYY*, January 23, 2022, https://billypenn.com/2022/01/23/a-1960s-state-official-claimed-pa-college-students-took-lsd-and-went-blind-and-newspapers-believed-him/

18 Sarah Boseley, "Prozac, Used by 40m People, Does Not Work Say Scientists," *Guardian*, 2008, https://www.theguardian.com/society/2008/feb/26/mentalhealth.medicalresearch

19 Kathleen Davis, "What Are the Uses of Ketamine?," *Medical News Today*, July 25, 2023, https://www.medicalnewstoday.com/articles/302663#what-is-it

20 Lauren Dunn, Kate Snow, "Ketamine Clinics for Mental Health Are Popping Up Across the U.S. Does the Treatment Work?," NBC News, January 4, 2023, https://www.nbcnews.com/health/mental-health/ketamine-clinics-mental-health-are-popping-us-treatment-work-rcna63522

21 Kirsten Grind, Katherine Bindley, "Magic Mushrooms. LSD. Ketamine. The Drugs That Power Silicon Valley," *The Wall Street Journal*, 2023, https://www.wsj.com/articles/silicon-valley-microdosing-ketamine-lsd-magic-mushrooms-d381e214

22 "20148 LSD," *CAMH*, https://www.camh.ca/en/health-info/mental-illness-and-addiction-index/lsd

23 "What Is LSD?," 2023, *ADF*, October 13, 2023, https://adf.org.au/drug-facts/lsd/

24 Ruairi J Mackenzie, "LSD for Anxiety: A Deep Dive into a New Clinical Trial," October 7, 2022, https://www.technologynetworks.com/neuroscience/articles/lsd-for-anxiety-a-deep-dive-into-a-new-clinical-trial-366381

25 "What Is MDMA?" 2017, *NIDA*, https://nida.nih.gov/publications/research-reports/mdma-ecstasy-abuse/what-mdma

26 "After Six-Decade Hiatus, Experimental Psychedelic Therapy Returns to the V.A.," *New York Times*, 2022, https://www.nytimes.com/2022/06/24/us/politics/psychedelic-therapy-veterans.html

27 Sarah Whelan, PhD., "Clinical Trial of DMT for Depression Announces 'Positive' Early Data," *Technology Networks*, April 6, 2023, https://www.technologynetworks.com/neuroscience/news/trial-of-dmt-for-depression-announces-positive-early-data-371933

28 David Gal, "Consumers Prefer Natural Medicines More When Treating Psychological than Physical Conditions," *SCP*, June 24, 2023, https://myscp.onlinelibrary.wiley.com/doi/abs/10.1002/jcpy.1371

29 "Mental Disorders," *WHO*, June 8, 2022, https://www.who.int/news-room/fact-sheets/detail/mental-disorders#:~:text=In%202019%2C%201%20in%20every,the%20most%20common%20(1).

30 Rachel Tompa, "5 Unsolved Mysteries About the Brain," *Allen Institute*, March 14, 2019, https://alleninstitute.org/news/5-unsolved-mysteries-about-the-brain/

31 Gabor Maté with Daniel Maté, *The Myth of Normal*, Avery, September 13, 2022.

32 "Mental Health Matters," *Lancet Global Health*, November 2020, https://www.thelancet.com/journals/langlo/article/PIIS2214-109X(20)30432-0/fulltext

33 Kirsten Grind, Katherine Bindley, "Magic Mushrooms. LSD. Ketamine. The Drugs That Power Silicon Valley," *The Wall Street Journal*, 2023, https://www.wsj.com/articles/silicon-valley-microdosing-ketamine-lsd-magic-mushrooms-d381e214

34 Jeremy Sutton, "5 Benefits of Journaling for Mental Health," May 14, 2018, https://positivepsychology.com/benefits-of-journaling/

35 "Mental Health Benefits of Journaling," October 25, 2021, *WebMD*, https://www.webmd.com/mental-health/mental-health-benefits-of-journaling

36 Nancy Olson, "Three Ways that Handwriting with a Pen Positively Affects Your Brain," *Forbes*, 2016, https://www.forbes.com/sites/nancyolson/2016/05/15/three-ways-that-writing-with-a-pen-positively-affects-your-brain/?sh=3cfaedb65705

37 "The Benefits of Handwriting vs. Typing," https://www.pens.com/blog/the-benefits-of-handwriting-vs-typing/

38 Lidija Globokar, The Power of Visualization and How to Use It," *Forbes*, March 5,2020, https://www.forbes.com/sites/lidijaglobokar/2020/03/05/the-power-of-visualization-and-how-to-use-it/?sh=163924bc6497

39 Marschall S. Runge, M.D., Ph.D. "Weighing the Facts: The Tough Truth About Weight Loss," *Michigan Medicine*, April 12, 2017, https://www.michiganmedicine.org/health-lab/weighing-facts-tough-truth-about-weight-loss

40 "Lottery Winners Who Won Millions but Ended up with Nothing," *Live Life Richer with Lovemoney*, 2021, https://www.lovemoney.com/galleries/64958/lottery-winners-who-won-millions-but-ended-up-with-nothing?page=1

41 "Mental Illness," *Mayo Clinic*, Mayo Foundation for Medical Education and Research, December 13, 2022, https://www.mayoclinic.org/diseases-conditions/mental-illness/symptoms-causes/syc-20374968

42 Nicole F. Roberts, "Rejection and Physical Pain Are the Same to Your Brain," December 15, 2015, https://www.forbes.com/sites/nicolefisher/2015/12/25/rejection-and-physical-pain-are-the-same-to-your-brain/?sh=1687f6e04f87

43 Dana Kanze, Laura Huang, Mark A. Conley, E. Tory Higgins, "Male and Female Entrepreneurs Get Asked Different Questions by VCs — and It Affects How Much Funding They Get," June 27, 2017, https://hbr.org/2017/06/male-and-female-entrepreneurs-get-asked-different-questions-by-vcs-and-it-affects-how-much-funding-they-get

Acknowledgments

A journey of a thousand miles begins with a single step; who is to say which one was the most important—the first, the last, another one? Accordingly, where do you start and where do you stop when acknowledging the people, situations, and events that helped you grow and manifest an idea into physical reality?

Many people who supported me along the way are not present in these acknowledgments. They might be a past teacher, frenemy, or boss.

To anyone who ever crossed my path, you have been instrumental in helping me become who I am.

"The flutter of a butterfly's wing can ultimately cause a typhoon halfway around the world."
—Aleatha Romig

Nonetheless, there are many people who specifically helped bring this book to life. I would like to acknowledge my partner, benefactor, husband, and supporter, Maxim Sytchev.

Deep gratitude goes out to my agent, Steve Carlis, and to my editor and dream team at Post Hill Press for making this book a reality. Thank you to Debra Englander, Caitlin Burdette, Aleigha, and Mindie Barnett.

A big thank you to my marketing agency, 2MM, my photographer, Jeremie Dupont, my hair and make-up artist Vanessa Baudner, and my graphic designer, Cass Creative.

Many thanks to all of my friends and cheerleaders who have been alongside me in the process. Your support has been priceless and I am very grateful for your presence.

I am deeply grateful for the collaboration with Lise Janelle, Pam Wright, Elham from Energy by Elham, and Isabelle from Health and Natural Life. You made me a better human!

To my family, I know that I am not always easy to follow and that our relationships have not always been the smoothest, but no matter what, our lives are forever intertwined.

To my childhood friends, regardless of the distance and time, you will always be in my heart.

And last but not least, a big thank you to my furry family, Oscar, Twinkle, and Bastet, for their unconditional love and teachings.

About the Author

photo credit:
Jeremie Dupont

After spending twenty years in the financial services and technology industries as an executive and a venture capitalist, Peggy Van de Plassche now speaks and writes about the benefits of alternative medicines, such as micro-dosing psilocybin, for professional and personal growth. She is the creator of *MORE — The Microdose Diet: The 90-Day Plan for More Success, Passion, and Happiness.*

A veteran public speaker, Peggy has participated in over fifty global events, from exclusive board meetings to premier industry conferences. She is active on social media, and you can follow her work on Substack, LinkedIn, Apple Podcast, and YouTube.